ROUTLEDGE LIBRARY EDITIONS:
ENERGY ECONOMICS

Volume 19

THE NIGERIAN OIL ECONOMY

THE NIGERIAN OIL ECONOMY
From Prosperity to Glut

J.K. ONOH

Routledge
Taylor & Francis Group

LONDON AND NEW YORK

First published in 1983 by Croom Helm Ltd

This edition first published in 2018
by Routledge
2 Park Square, Milton Park, Abingdon, Oxon OX14 4RN

and by Routledge
711 Third Avenue, New York, NY 10017

Routledge is an imprint of the Taylor & Francis Group, an informa business

British Library Cataloguing in Publication Data
A catalogue record for this book is available from the British Library

ISBN: 978-1-138-10476-1 (Set)
ISBN: 978-1-315-14526-6 (Set) (ebk)
ISBN: 978-1-138-30794-0 (Volume 19) (hbk)
ISBN: 978-1-315-14298-2 (Volume 19) (ebk)

Publisher's Note
The publisher has gone to great lengths to ensure the quality of this reprint but points out that some imperfections in the original copies may be apparent.

Disclaimer
The publisher has made every effort to trace copyright holders and would welcome correspondence from those they have been unable to trace.

The Nigerian Oil Economy

From Prosperity to Glut

J.K. Onoh

CROOM HELM
London & Canberra

ST. MARTIN'S PRESS
New York

© 1983 J.K. Onoh
Croom Helm Ltd, Provident House, Burrell Row,
Beckenham, Kent BR3 1AT
Croom Helm Australia, PO Box 391,
Manuka, ACT 2603, Australia

British Library Cataloguing in Publication Data

Onoh, J.K.
    The Nigerian Oil Economy.
    1. Petroleum industry and trade — Nigeria
    2. Nigeria — Economic conditions
    I. Title
    338.2'72'8209669   HC1055

    ISBN 0-7099-1901-8

All rights reserved. For information, write:
St. Martin's Press, Inc., 175 Fifth Avenue, New York, N.Y. 10010
Printed in Great Britain
First published in the United States of America in 1983

Library of Congress Cataloging in Publication Data

Onoh, J.K.
    The Nigerian Oil Economy.

    Includes index.
    1. Petroleum industry and trade — Nigeria — History.
2. Investments, Foreign — Nigeria — History. 3. Nigeria —
Economic conditions — 1960-   . I. Title.
HD9577.N52056   1983   338.2'7282'09669   83-4577
ISBN 0-312-57274-3

Typeset by Leaper & Gard Ltd, Bristol
Printed and bound in Great Britain
by Billing & Sons Limited, Worcester.

CONTENTS

TABLES AND FIGURES

Tables

Figures

PREFACE

Although Nigeria is rated as the world's tenth largest producer of oil, little information is available on the implications of oil production for the Nigerian economy. This book is intended to synthesise the scattered information into an integrated framework and provide information on oil in the Nigerian economy for both Nigerians and the international community. This book is especially relevant in the eighties, which has been characterised by a world oil glut and the search for energy substitutes.

Until 1960 Nigeria was little known as a world producer of oil. She was known rather as a producer of cash crops such as palm produce, groundnut, cocoa, cotton and timber and her export earnings depended on these products. Then suddenly Nigeria became a world producer of oil and the traditional sources of income were neglected. Policy-makers paid lip service to the diversification of Nigeria's economy and relied heavily on oil revenue for carrying out the country's development programmes, for the payment of imports and for settling international debt obligations. Nigeria's external reserves increased in leaps and bounds. Government expenditure rose astronomically and Nigerians spent freely at home and abroad. Business apparently flourished.

In the mid-seventies economic indicators began to warn of the danger of Nigeria's reliance on oil income alone. But these warnings about the consequences of over-reliance on oil monies for Nigeria's economic development and the dangers of non-diversification of Nigeria's economy fell on deaf ears. By 1980, the Nigerian economy had reached crisis point. All direct and indirect instruments of economic control, ranging from restrictive monetary, banking and fiscal measures to direct interventions, were put into full gear to salvage the situation. Incriminations and recriminations were made. Nigerians blamed the policy-makers of the Nigerian economy — the Government, while the Government blamed international conspiracy.

The book examines the role played by oil in the Nigerian economy as well as the position of Nigeria in OPEC. It will certainly be of interest to Nigerian and international policy-makers, to those whose businesses to a large extent depend on oil, to students of petroleum economics, business and international finance and to those interested in world power politics as they affect Third World countries.

I am very much indebted to the Imo State University Research Grant Committee which provided me with a research grant for the purpose of preparing this book. By this gesture, the Imo State University has lived up to the aims of its founding fathers of finding practical answers to contemporary problems — an ideal which is neatly enshrined in the Institution's motto, 'Excellence and Service'. It is hoped that the findings of this book will be of service to Nigerian policy makers and of benefit to the Nigerian nation.

I am also indebted to the Public Affairs Department of the Nigerian National Petroleum Corporation (NNPC) for the various publications it made available to me and to the Library of the Central Bank of Nigeria, with which I have been very closely associated and which in the past provided me with material support for my earlier books.

J.K. Onoh,
Imo State University,
Aba Campus,
Nigeria.

1 MULTINATIONALS IN THE NIGERIAN ECONOMY

Multinationals, transnationals or international financial conglomerates are large firms which are characterised by large capital
outlay, abundance of technological know-how, a variety of technical
and managerial manpower and efficiency in the pursuit of profit. In
the developing economies of Africa, Asia and Latin America, where
the spirit of nationalism is still very much alive, multinationals are
regarded as the agents of neocolonialism whose sole objective is to
exploit the resources of the developing economies to the advantage of
their native countries.

Multinationals began operations in the area now known as Nigeria
long before Nigeria became a political entity. Although the area was
ceded to the British in 1885 as a colony by the Treaty of Berlin, which
partitioned Africa among the European powers, Nigeria only
became a political entity in 1914, when the Northern and Southern
provinces of Nigeria were amalgamated by Lord Lugard. Before
1914, some multinationals in banking and commercial spheres had
already established themselves in Nigeria. For example, the African
Banking Corporation (ABC) began operations in Lagos in 1891,
while the Royal Niger Company, which traded in palm produce along
the Nigerian coast, was established in 1886.

Until Nigeria became independent in 1960 only British companies
or those of British dominions or protectorates and those of other
Western nations duly permitted by the British authorities were
allowed to do business in Nigeria. With the attainment of independence in 1960 the Nigerian goverment and people became worried
about the economic and political implications of doing business with
British companies only. As a number of advantages could be derived
by opening up trade links with other countries of the world, the policy
of multilateral economic relationships with the rest of the world was
adopted. Nigeria therefore began to do business with companies
from Western Europe, the United States, Commonwealth and Asian
countries and the Socialist countries.

This chapter will examine the aggregate activities of multinationals
operating in the Nigerian economy as summarised by the total investments from their countries of origin. It was only after Nigeria's

1

political independence in 1960 that it became possible to keep a fairly good record of the activities of foreign companies in Nigeria and the nations from which such companies originated. Such records became necessary for planning purposes and for defining the strength of economic and political relationships between Nigeria and those countries.

1. Growth and Decline of Foreign Investments in Nigeria

Table 1.1 suggests strongly that the United Kingdom still leads other countries of the world in terms of total investments of multinationals operating in Nigeria. In 1962 the total investments made in Nigeria by multinationals of UK origin totalled ₦271.2 million or approximately 61.4 per cent of total foreign investments in Nigeria. By 1967 cumulative British investments in Nigeria had declined to 47.1 per cent, but this decline of British investments in Nigeria after Nigeria's independence is understandable. With the attainment of independence, Nigerian businessmen became more enterprising. The bureaucratic bottlenecks which had hindered their operations during the colonial era were reduced. Business licences and registrations became easy to obtain. Various incentives were provided. Bank loans became more readily available than they were before independence. The predominant British banks in the past considered Nigerian businessmen as risky borrowers. The liberalisation of bank credit partly explains the decline in total British investment in Nigeria. Another factor which contributed to the decline was the new policy of multilateral economic relationships with the rest of the world. The new policy threw the Nigerian economic door wide open to other foreign investors which hitherto were unable to gain access to Nigerian markets because of restrictive colonial, economic and trade policies.

The cumulative UK investments in Nigeria in 1967 were much higher than those of 1962. But in terms of overall foreign investment, British investments declined in percentage terms. Obviously, the increase in the United States' investments in Nigeria from 8.7 per cent of aggregate foreign investments in 1962 to 23.6 per cent of total foreign investments in 1967 contributed in no small way to the decline in the United Kingdom's aggregate investments in Nigeria by 1967. However by 1973 United States' investments in Nigeria had

Table 1.1: Cumulative Foreign Investment in Nigeria by Country or Region of Origin (₦ million)

Country or Region	1962 Actual and % of total foreign investment		1967 Actual and % of total foreign investment		1973 Actual and % of total foreign investment		1977 Actual and % of total foreign investment	
United Kingdom	271.2	(61.4%)	366.0	(47.1%)	860.9	(48.8%)	1072.8	(42.37%)
United States	38.8	(8.7%)	183.2	(23.6%)	308.0	(17.5%)	287.2	(11.33%)
Western Europe (excluding UK)	93.6	(21.2%)	164.8	(21.2%)	415.2	(23.5%)	739.0	(29.20%)
Others	38.2	(8.7%)	63.0	(8.1%)	179.6	(10.2%)	432.4	(17.10)
TOTAL	441.8	(100%)	777.0	(100%)	1,763.7	(100%)	2531.4	(100%)

Source: Central Bank of Nigeria, *Economic and Financial Review* (various issues).

declined to 17.5 per cent, while those of the UK increased slightly to 48.8 per cent in the same year.

The decline in the United States' investments in Nigeria by 1973 may be attributed to a number of causes. A major factor was the recession in the US economy which started in the mid-1960s and the persistent deficit in the US balance of payments, coupled with the devaluation of the dollar in 1973 arising from dollar pressure on the international foreign exchange markets. The Nigeria/Biafra war which lasted from mid-1967 to January 1970 damaged Nigeria's investment climate. New investors were scared away, while some investors already operating in the Nigerian economy panicked and left. From 1973 United States' investments in Nigeria began to decline as well as those of the United Kingdom although US investments declined at a much faster rate than those of the UK which in 1977 amounted to 42.37 per cent of total foreign investments in Nigeria while that of the US constituted only 11.33 per cent. The investments of West European countries have on the other hand maintained a steady growth from 1962, especially investments from France and West Germany. Asian investments, particularly those of Japan, Taiwan, Korea and India have also shown some remarkable increases since 1973. In 1977 the total investments of countries classified as 'others' under which Asian investments and those of Commonwealth and Socialist countries are considered stood at 17.10 per cent of total foreign investments.

2. Capital Holdings of Foreign and Indigenous Investors in the Nigerian Economy

Since the 1970s there has been a remarkable increase in the volume of investments of Nigerian indigenes *vis à vis* foreign investors. Between 1914, when Nigeria became a political entity under the British administration and 1960, when Nigeria became politically independent, most investments in Nigeria were of UK origin or those of non-UK origin permitted to operate in the country during the colonial period. Until 1960 over 90 per cent of total investments in Nigeria were under foreign ownership. However, from 1966 Nigerian investors began to make incursions into the Nigerian economy. Within a decade the percentage of cumulative paid-up capital of Nigerians rose from 0.9 per cent in 1966 to 43 per cent in 1977. The developments are shown in Table 1.2. By 1970 Nigerian

Table 1.2: Cumulative Paid-up Capital[a] Holdings of
Foreigners and Nigerians in the Nigerian Economy
(₦ thousands)

Year	Held by Foreigners		Held by Nigerians	
	₦	%	₦	%
1966	225,648	(92.1)	19,474	(0.9)
1967	229,146	(91.2)	22,172	(1.8)
1968	238,742	(90.6)	24,762	(9.4)
1969	249,938	(80.9)	59,146	(9.1)
1970	259,736	(81.2)	60,108	(18.8)
1971	287,932	(83.4)	57,426	(16.6)
1972	304,238	(75.5)	98,688	(24.6)
1973	340,459	(68.5)	156,376	(31.5)
1974	301,095	(57.7)	220,601	(42.3)
1975	331,371	(56.6)	253,994	(43.4)
1976	397,365	(59.4)	272,152	(40.6)
1977	432,763	(57.0)	325,249	(43.0)

Note: a. Excluding reserves in the Nigerian economy.

Source: Central Bank of Nigeria, *Economic and Financial Reviews* (various issues).

investors had less than 20 per cent of the total paid-up capital in the form of common stocks or preferred stocks, excluding reserves in the Nigerian economy. In 1972 the Nigerian Military Government promulgated the *Nigerian Enterprises Promotions Decree* (now Act), which made it mandatory for foreign investors to sell a part of their business to Nigerians and to indigenise their manpower resources. Under the Decree, businesses which were classified under Schedule I such as printing, retail trade, light industries, advertising, public relations, estate agencies etc., were reserved exclusively for Nigerians. Schedule II of the Decree permitted foreigners to own up to 40 per cent equity participation in such activities as brewery, insurance, fertiliser production, food processing, distribution and maintenance of motor vehicles; detergent industry, book publications, etc. Under Schedule III foreigners were allowed to own up to 60 per cent of the equity capital. Relatively heavy and capital intensive industries fall under Schedule III of the Decree. Activities under Schedule III are considered capital intensive and at times beyond the capacity of Nigerian private investors to mobilise the required capital for starting and operating such industries.

Following the Enterprises Promotions Decree there was a significant increase in Nigerian ownership of paid-up capital. From 18.8 per cent in 1970, Nigerian ownership of capital rose to 43 per cent in 1977.

Although Nigerians hold on average a total investment of 43 per cent consisting of common and preferred stocks, an appraisal of the capital holdings of Nigerians in the various activities of the economy is not very encouraging. Table 1.3 shows a breakdown of the percentage capital holdings of foreigners and Nigerians in the various activities of the Nigerian economy. As of 1977, the last year in which statistics were available, foreigners still controlled over 50 per cent of capital holdings in manufacturing and processing activities; agriculture, forestry and fishery; building and construction; trading and business services and miscellaneous activities. It is only in mining and quarrying, and transportation and communication that Nigerians control about 60 per cent of the capital holdings of those activities.

In mining and quarrying activities Nigerian capital holdings have increased astronomically since 1974 because of changes in Nigerian oil policies which made it possible for the Nigerian Federal Government to participate actively in oil exploitation and exploration instead of the old oil policy in which Nigeria benefited from rents and royalties only under concessional agreements. Nigerians have always participated in transport activities especially road, rail and air transport. The 39 per cent foreign capital holdings in the transport and communication sector is mainly in the area of communication.

Unfortunately, activities in such important areas as agriculture, forestry and fishery, and manufacturing and processing are still in foreign hands. These activities are fundamental to any developing economy. A country which depends on foreign investors for her food production is not worth her name because if such foreigners pull out their investments the nation will starve. Manufacturing and processing activties are very important activities for developing ecnomies eager to industrialise. Manufacturing and processing industries provide rudimentary transfer of technology, technical and managerial manpower training and forward and backward linkage effects to any economy. The inability of Nigerians to participate actively in these areas does not augur well for the country. In 1970 Nigerian investors controlled 42.7 per cent of total investments in manufacturing and processing activities. By 1977, it had risen to only 46 per cent. In building and construction, trading and business services and miscellaneous activities foreign investors still have the upper hand. Building and construction activities are capital intensive; they also require a reasonably high level of technical know-how which Nigeria does not yet possess in abundance. The big names in the construction industry are foreign such as Julius Berger, Fougerole, Guffanti, MCC, Cappa and Dalberto, Michelleti, etc. Trading and business services are still controlled by foreigners who have access to foreign exchange restricted to Nigerians. Foreigners still have the upper hand especially in banking and insurance services. In these industries foreigners still control over 50 per cent of banking and insurance capital. It is in the activity of trading and business services that foreigners have the highest capital holdings.

3. Recent Changes in Overall Foreign Investments in Nigeria

Since 1972 (the year the Nigerian Enterprises Promotion Decree came into force) there has been a reasonable decline in the annual percentage change of Nigeria's foreign private capital with the exception of 1975 (see Table 1.4). Worldwide inflation and turbulence in the foreign exchange market eroded the purchasing power of Nigeria's external reserves. The depreciation in the value of external reserves adversely affected the foreign exchange content of domestic investments, especially in mining and quarrying; building and construction; trading and business services; and agriculture, forestry and fishery and in fact virtually all economic activities. Since 1975 there have been sudden upsurges in total cumulative foreign investments notably in mining and quarrying, manufacturing and processing and in trading and business services. By 1977 the annual percentage change in total cumulative foreign investments had declined from the 26.3 per cent level of 1975 to 8.4 per cent in 1977.

While capital flows into Nigeria it also flows out of Nigeria for reasons best known to investors. Table 1.5 shows the flow of foreign private capital in Nigeria. It suggests strongly that Nigeria is still on the gaining side, but the severe fluctuations in foreign capital flow may be attributed partly to changes in Nigerian investment policies and partly to the general world ecnomic recession. There is therefore a great need to mobilise domstic capital in the Nigerian economy and to harness scarce foreign exchange by reducing imports. By reducing the imports of non essential and luxury goods, Nigeria will be able to conserve enough foreign exchange to support the foreign exchange contents of domestic investments.

Table 1.3: Cumulative Percentage Capital[a] Holdings of Foreigners and Nigerians in the Nigerian Economy Classified According to Economic Activities

Years	1966		1967		1968		1969		1970		1971	
Nature of Holding (%)	F	N	F	N	F	N	F	N	F	N	F	N
Mining and Quarrying	100	—	100	—	100	—	100	—	100	—	100	—
Manufacturing and Processing	81.4	19.6	80.0	20.0	81.0	19.0	59.3	40.7	57.3	42.3	65.7	34.3
Agriculture, Forestry and Fishery	81.9	18.1	71.0	29.0	59.3	40.7	76.8	23.2	57.4	42.6	81.6	18.4
Transport and Communication	19.4	79.6	19.4	79.6	13.1	86.9	45.9	54.1	50.2	49.8	68.2	31.8
Trading and Business Services	99.0	11.0	98.9	1.1	98.6	1.4	96.4	3.6	94.2	5.8	99.9	0.1
Miscellaneous	57.0	43.0	36.9	43.1	59.5	40.5	91.0	9.0	84.3	15.7	83.4	16.6

Nature of Holding (%)	1972 F	1972 N	1973 F	1973 N	1974 F	1974 N	1975 F	1975 N	1976 F	1976 N	1977 F	1977 N
Mining and Quarrying	98.3	1.7	65.0	35.0	41.3	58.7	37.6	72.4	39.2	69.8	40.8	59.2
Manufacturing and Processing	57.0	43.0	58.4	41.6	59.0	41.0	52.7	47.3	56.7	43.3	54.0	46.0
Agriculture, Forestry and Fishery	82.8	17.2	81.7	18.3	53.9	46.1	63.6	36.4	69.7	30.3	64.8	35.2
Transport and Communication	73.2	26.8	58.1	41.9	45.8	54.2	40.0	60.0	43.1	56.9	39.0	61.0
Trading and Business Services	41.2	58.8	72.2	27.8	86.1	13.9	73.5	26.5	75.3	24.7	72.3	27.7
Miscellaneous	75.5	24.5	68.5	31.5	57.7	42.3	62.3	37.7	62.7	37.3	55.0	45.0

Notes: a. Common and preferred stock.
F = Foreign holdings of capital (affiliate parent Company + non-resident holdings).
N = Nigerian holdings of capital.

Source: Extracted from CBN, *Economic and Financial Review* (various issues).

In the First Development Plan (1962/8) the total planned capital formation was ₦2,367 million whereby the total financing expected from abroad was ₦1,049 million or 44 per cent of Nigeria's total planned capital formation. Out of the expected ₦1,049 million from abroad, ₦396 million constituted foreign investment while ₦653 million constituted foreign aid. In the Second Development Plan (1970/4) the total planned capital formation was ₦3,190 million, whereby total financing from abroad was estimated at ₦1,127 million or 35 per cent of total capital formation. Foreign investment rose to ₦825 million as against ₦396 million in the First Plan period. On the other hand foreign aid declined to ₦302 million as against ₦653 million in the First Plan period.

In the First and Second Development Plan periods growth rates of 4 per cent and 6.6 per cent per annum were projected respectively. The Third Development Plan covered the period from 1975 to 1980. The last Plan did not envisage any foreign investment or foreign aid for its realisation, although the 1976 financial statistics have shown evidence of foreign capital flow into Nigeria even though it was discounted in the capital projection upon which the realisation of the growth rate of 9 per cent per annum depended. The 1981/5 Plan also relies heavily on domestic financing sources. The prospect has been dimmed by the world oil glut which has led to a reduction in the Nigerian output of oil. This unexpected turn of events has affected quite adversely Nigeria's oil proceeds and the prosecution of the Plan. As of April, 1982, the Nigerian daily oil production quota has reduced by a half following the Quito OPEC Conference of March, 1982. Nigeria's critical oil export position has been exacerbated by the decision of the British Oil Company to reduce the price of North Sea oil to 31 dollars per barrel, about five dollars below Nigeria's price for the same grade of oil. Major international oil producing companies have threatened to abandon Nigerian crude for North Sea oil. But OPEC has also threatened to blacklist oil companies which abandon the purchase of Nigerian oil. To ameliorate cash flow, Saudi Arabia is said to have offered Nigeria a 'soft' loan of one billion dollars to help overcome its pressing crises.

But Nigeria will continue to need foreign investments and, quite probably, foreign aid as well. Nigeria has already approached the World Bank for assistance as oil can no longer be relied upon for the long-term growth of the Nigerian economy.

4. Reservations Against the Operations of Foreign Investors in the Nigerian Economy

The feelings against the operations of multinationals in Nigeria are not different from those expressed in other countries of the Third World. A high level of industrialisation notwithstanding, West European countries such as the UK, France and West Germany are worried about the level of American investments in their countries, especially the political and economic implications. The developing countries are even more worried about the presence of multinationals in their dependent economies which are very far from the level of development achieved by Western Europe. The fear is deep-seated that the politics of a country, in which the economy is overwhelmingly controlled by multinationals, will be invariably controlled directly or indirectly by either the multinationals or the country of origin of such multinationals. No country can afford to hand over its political and economic destinies to outside control and still speak of political sovereignty. If multinationals are allowed to control the economy of any country then such multinationals become the *de facto* policy-making body of that country, deciding the level of investment to be made, the level of output to be attained in the economy, the structure of wages and salaries, the level of employment and the overall social development of that country. Should the multinationals cease to operate for reasons of low profitability then the economy will be paralysed. A political vacuum is created and anarchy will become the order of the day in the course of the power tussle between nationals to fill the vacuum. It is in the light of the above that strong reservations have been expressed in many countries about the operations of multinationals in developing economies. The consequences of unrestricted operations of multinationals in a developing economy in particular will be examined in two perspectives.

(a) Political Perspectives

Experiences the world over suggest beyond doubt that multinationals have influenced or attempted to influence the political institutions of the countries in which they operate. Developing countries are more vulnerable in this respect, as they possess little experience in the supposedly Machiavellian art of statecraft and their leaders have little knowledge of international power politics and diplomacy. Multinationals on the other hand are adepts in political power brokerage,

Table 1.4: Cumulative Foreign Investment by Type of Activity (₦ million)

Year	Mining and Quarrying	Manufacturing and Processing	Agriculture, Forestry and Fishery	Transport and Communication	Building and Construction	Trading and Business Services	Other Activities	Total	Annual % change
1962	162.0	76.6	8.6	4.8	17.0	169.8	3.0	441.8	17.1
1963	187.0	98.6	9.8	5.2	21.8	192.8	2.4	517.6	24.4
1964	258.0	117.2	10.8	7.0	24.6	202.4	23.6	643.6	17.1
1965	329.4	139.0	11.2	11.6	40.2	185.6	37.0	754.0	13.1
1966	425.0	149.0	9.6	13.0	19.0	211.6	25.6	852.8	8.9
1967	356.4	173.0	9.6	8.4	19.0	192.6	18.0	777.0	9.4
1968	417.2	169.8	9.6	9.6	19.8	205.8	28.2	850.0	3.7
1969	389.6	196.0	11.0	11.4	22.2	231.0	20.4	881.6	13.8
1970	515.4	224.8	11.2	13.8	13.8	206.6	17.6	1,003.2	31.9
1971	694.0	378.8	15.4	12.0	15.4	187.2	20.0	1,322.8	18.8
1972	859.7	356.6	9.4	12.2	34.3	242.7	56.2	1,571.1	12.25
1973	925.3	409.0	7.9	11.6	45.0	294.7	70.2	1,763.7	2.7
1974	818.1	520.4	20.7	21.9	64.2	321.3	45.5	1,812.1	26.34
1975	959.6	506.2	19.2	22.8	111.2	572.4	96.1	2,287.5	16.0
1976	918.9	550.7	21.9	11.0	122.5	624.8	84.0	2,335.8	8.4
1977	1,090.8	703.8	75.0	30.6	121.4	365.5	144.3	2,531.4	

Source: Central Bank of Nigeria, *Economic and Financial Review*, vol. 6, no. 2, December 1968; vol. 14, no. 1, March 1976; and vol. 17, no. 2, December 1979.

Table 1.5: Flow of Foreign Private Capital by Country of Origin (₦ million)

	United Kingdom			United States			Western Europe (excluding UK)			Others (unspecified)			Total		
	Inflow	Outflow	Net flow	Inflow	Outflow	Net flow	Inflow	Outflow	Net flow	Inflow	Outflow	Net flow	Inflow	Outflow	Net flow
1961	32.8	5.2	+ 27.6	14.4	2.6	+ 11.8	13.6	1.8	+ 11.8	3.4	—	+ 3.4	64.2	9.6	+ 54.6
1962	16.8	11.0	+ 5.8	9.0	1.0	+ 8.0	15.2	1.4	+ 13.8	8.8	1.0	+ 7.8	49.8	14.4	+ 35.4
1963	45.8	11.8	+ 34.0	13.4	2.6	+ 10.8	28.8	2.0	+ 26.8	4.4	0.2	+ 4.2	92.4	16.6	+ 75.8
1964	99.4	43.4	+ 56.0	32.8	2.8	+ 30.0	36.2	5.6	+ 30.6	13.6	4.2	+ 9.4	182.0	56.0	+ 126.0
1965	105.6	63.6	+ 42.0	39.6	2.2	+ 37.4	47.8	27.2	+ 21.6	13.0	3.6	+ 9.4	206.0	95.6	+ 110.4
1966	101.0	49.8	+ 51.2	16.2	1.8	+ 14.4	47.4	20.2	+ 27.2	9.2	3.2	+ 6.0	173.8	75.0	+ 98.8
1967	33.4	41.6	− 8.2	59.4	3.0	+ 56.4	9.8	10.4	+ 0.6	4.4	8.6	− 4.2	107.0	63.6	+ 43.4
1968	68.0	27.2	+ 40.8	18.8	0.4	+ 18.4	11.6	5.8	+ 5.8	8.0	—	+ 8.0	106.4	33.4	+ 73.0
1969	36.2	46.0	− 9.8	56.2	54.2	+ 2.0	39.4	14.8	+ 24.6	18.8	4.0	+ 14.8	150.6	119.0	+ 31.6
1970	94.6	47.2	+ 47.4	74.6	48.2	+ 26.4	58.0	28.4	+ 29.6	23.8	5.6	+ 18.2	251.0	129.7	+ 129.6
1971	207.2	59.6	+ 147.6	151.4	44.0	+ 107.4	92.6	56.4	+ 36.2	38.4	10.0	+ 28.4	489.6	170.0	+ 319.6
1972	236.0	58.3	+ 177.7	17.1	67.8	− 50.7	150.9	44.9	+ 106.0	28.8	13.5	+ 15.3	432.8	184.5	+ 248.3
1973	265.8	174.6	+ 91.2	174.3	153.0	+ 21.3	91.7	43.5	+ 48.2	46.9	14.1	+ 31.9	577.8	385.2	+ 192.6
1974	119.7	147.8	− 28.1	151.1	159.0	− 7.9	172.6	128.0	+ 44.6	63.7	24.0	+ 39.7	507.1	458.8	+ 48.3
1975	214.2	189.5	+ 24.7	253.0	17.8	+ 235.2	191.6	61.3	+ 130.3	98.6	13.4	+ 85.2	757.4	282.0	+ 475.4
1976	205.6	121.1	+ 84.5	39.0	198.0	− 159.0	195.8	132.9	+ 62.9	80.7	22.8	+ 57.9	521.1	474.8	+ 46.3
1977	320.0	189.2	+ 130.8	81.9	170.9	− 89.0	213.6	127.7	+ 85.9	101.8	31.9	+ 69.9	717.3	519.7	+ 197.6

Source: Central Bank of Nigeria, *Economic and Financial Review* vol. 6, no. 2, December, 1968; vol. 14, no. 1, March, 1976; and vol. 17, no. 2, December, 1979.

neutralisation and the use of labour unions against the host governments.

Where the host government is installed through the machinations
of multinationals it is rendered *ab initio* ineffective in both domestic
and international politics. The policies of the government become
subordinate to those of the multinationals. Where the leader of such a
country assumes power through the democratic process, he is persuaded to adjust to the desires of multinationals or his technocrats
may come under their manipulations so that policies conducive to the
operations of the multinationals are made. Through bribery and
other forms of corrupt practices, including paid overseas leave, multinationals worm themselves into positions of power in the policy-
making machinery of the host country. In Nigeria there has been
evidence of such corrupt practices by multinationals. The Crude
Sales Oil Tribunal scandal of 1980, the Lockheed Plane scandal, the
Multimillion naira Swiss-bus scandal and the Leyland Trucks scandal
are still very fresh in the minds of Nigerians. Prominent Nigerian
nationals in positions of power and multinationals operating in
Nigeria collaborated in these recent scandals.

The legal and political institutions of many developing countries
lack the experience and machinery for coping with the activities of
multinationals. There are no correct statistics of the number of multinationals operating in the developing countries, and their levels of
operation. In contract bids and agreement preparations, multinationals always succeed in outwitting the developing countries
especially in the sophisticated areas of manufacturing and mineral
exploration. In some countries powerful multinationals are known to
have insisted on immunity for their workers from any form of legal
prosecution in the host country. Where a country has no option it is
forced into building immunity from prosecution into the contract
agreement with the multinationals.

Because of inefficiency in the tax machineries of most developing
countries and the corruptible nature of most of the poorly-paid tax
assessment officials, some multinationals influence tax assessors and
end up paying little tax to the treasury of the host government. In
some cases, multinationals evade taxes entirely because of the
undeveloped nature of the tax laws which in some developing
countries make the non-payment of taxes a civil, rather than a
criminal, offence.

Multinationals have also been criticised in their social policies,
which have been termed discriminatory to the people of the host

country, and which cause social tension between the people of the host country, the government and the multinationals themselves. For example, some multinationals establish their own quarters and facilities which are restricted for the use of foreign nationals and to the exclusion of nationals of comparable status with their foreign counterparts. While foreign workers of multinationals live in luxurious quarters, and often own swimming pools and games facilities nationals engaged in senior management or technical positions are excluded from owning such facilities. While the children of foreign nationals of multinationals attend first-class schools established by the multinationals, the children of the workers of the host country are excluded from attending such schools. Many multinationals have been accused of spending a large proportion of their capital for the comfort of their foreign workers to the detriment of revenue which should accrue to the host country in the form of taxes. Increased operational costs also reduce the profit margin which multinationals share with their host partners under profit-sharing partnership agreements.

Naturally no sovereign nation can afford to lose her national pride to foreign operators. A country which is not in control of its own economy can hardly be respected at an international level and the pronouncements of such a country can hardly be taken seriously. The ability of a country to control its economy is an important parameter when measuring that country's international standing.

(b) Economic Perspectives

Foreign multinationals operate in developing countries in various forms: as direct investors owning 100 per cent of the equity capital in an enterprise; or in partnerships with the government of the host country, or with nationals of the host country. Others operate in areas of contract finance or suppliers' credit. Under contractor-finance schemes, the government of a country or its agencies (or a state government as in the case of Nigeria) enters into an agreement with a foreign contractor to construct and equip a project from the contractor's own resources. The period of repayment is agreed and a high interest rate of about 10 per cent per annum or more is charged. Under the supplier-credit scheme on the other hand, the equipment is sold to the government or its agencies by the foreign supplier and at a rate of interest a little lower than that scheduled for contractor-finance schemes. The contractor is guaranteed a repayment against any loss or damage of the said equipment in the event of political or economic crises. Supplier credit operates in the form of export guaranteed schemes of the importing government and the financial institutions of the supplying country. Supplier credit and contractor finance are normally guaranteed by the government against default in payment.

In most cases the supplier of the equipment is also the manufacturer and the financier of the equipment. Sometimes the regulations of the supplying country may demand that the equipment supplied under contractor finance or supplier credit be freighted in the carrier of the supplying country and that the installation be carried out by the technicians of the supplier and sometimes at rates which are obviously exorbitant. Because of the ignorance of the importing country, suppliers may sometimes bring in equipment or plant which is outdated or expensive, or which has no bearing on the capital/labour ratio considered relevant for the proper development of the economy. Cases also abound where a developing country is talked into starting certain projects which were not initially part of the country's development plan. The developing country is forced into accepting the proposed project if only to fulfil election promises about starting an industry or industries.

Multinationals operating as contractor-financiers and suppliers of credit often operate outside the developing countries in which they have dealings. The exorbitant interest charges, the shortness of the repayment period coupled with the multiplicity of viable and unviable projects impose a tremendous pressure on the foreign services of a developing country, distort balance of payments and put pressure on the debt service ratio, i.e., the ratio of debt service payments (interest charges and amortisation) to current account receipts — and finally endanger the ratio of public debt service payments to government revenue.

When the external reserves of a country are under pressure, a country's domestic currency becomes overvalued and inflation rages. Investments shift from direct productive activities to indirect activities, such as the importation of consumer goods. In the absence of rigorous import restrictions or controls the propensity to import further aggravates the precarious foreign exchange reserves positions of developing countries. While credit suppliers and contract financiers operate mostly from their countries' bases, others are registered or incorporated in the country in which they do business. All multinationals are primarily motivated by the quest for profit. Multinationals therefore tend to engage themselves in those economic activities which lead to a quick realisation of that primary objective. Businesses with a quick turnover, such as wholesale and distributive trades, are the main interest areas of some multinationals. Before the Nigerian Enterprises Promotion Decree of 1972, multinationals controlled most trade and business services in Nigeria. Activities which do not bring quick turnover such as transportation or cash crop production are not the first choice of many multinationals.

Technical and managerial know-how are hardly transferred willingly by multinationals to the developing countries. Consequently the advantages of technological gains are lost to the developing countries in which the multinationals operate. Until recently the highest training received by indigenes serving under multinationals in some countries were of the middle-manpower levels. Because of the indigenisation programme which began in 1972 foreign companies operating in Nigeria are now forced to Nigerianise their operations, especially in those enterprises which fall under Schedules II and III of the Decree in which foreign companies were required to sell a part of their shares and form partnerships with Nigerians. Intensive programmes of middle and high level manpower training schemes have begun to ensure that efficiency in operations continues to be maintained in order to protect the investments of foreigners and their Nigerian partners.

Another aspect of the operation of foreign companies which has received serious criticism in Nigeria is the use of local officials or workers to cheat the economy. For example, through collusion between Nigerian nationals and foreign companies, unethical practices such as the overpricing of imported equipment and raw materials are common. Through overpricing of equipment and raw materials more costs are incurred which are indirectly transferred as profits to the parent company of the Nigerian-based multinationals. The oil companies, for example, are known for their speedy amortisation of expensive oil drilling equipment so that fresh orders may be placed. Through quick replacement of equipment the tied shops of the oil companies in Europe and America are kept active in terms of employment and, of course, profits.

The Nigerian economic squeeze of 1982 was mainly blamed on the drop in oil prices and a reduction in oil production quotas. The straw which broke the back of the Nigerian economy is said to be smuggling and foreign companies are suspected to have abetted smuggling in Nigeria by illegally importing goods into the country through the use of private jetties benevolently leased to them to facilitate the discharge of equipment and raw materials required by the industries of foreign companies. There are more than 200 private jetties scattered around the ports and coasts of Nigeria whose uses have been grossly abused by nationals and multinationals. The container system which was designed to facilitate off-loading and clearance of goods of foreign and Nigerian companies has also been abused. Exporters are known to have colluded with their Nigerian agents to consign illegal goods or falsify documents relating to such goods. Luxury cars, machinery and other consumer items for which high duties are normally charged are known to have been cleared as biscuits or rice for which little or no duties are paid.

The experience gained as a result of foreign companies operating in Nigeria has been most rewarding. Nigerians and Nigerian governments have learnt, at times at great cost, the act of planning, organisation, control and co-ordination of business activities. These experiences have been particularly helpful in the more complex business of the oil industry, which will form the crux of the remaining chapters of this book.

References and Additional Reading

Brockway, F., *African Socialism*, Dufour Editions, Chester Springs, Pennsylvania, 1963

Brooke, M. and Remmers, H., *The Strategy of Multinational Enterprise*, American Elsevier Co., New York, 1979

Buchanan, N.S., *International Investment and Domestic Welfare*, New York, 1945

Central Bank of Nigeria, 'Foreign Private Investment in 1976 and 1977', in *Economic and Financial Review*, vol. 17, no. 2, Dec., 1979

Friedland, W.H. and Rosberg, C.G., *African Socialism*, Standford University Press, Standford, California, 1965

Hirschman, A.O., 'Obstacles to Economic Development: A Classification and a Quasi-Vanishing Act', *Economic Development and Cultural Change*, vol. XIII, no. 4, Part 1, July, 1965

Jacoby, Neil H., *Multinational Oil*, Macmillan Publishing Company, Inc., New York, 1974

Kamanu, O.S., *Nigeria and the Multinationals: Challenge and Response*, presented at the Conference on the 'New International Economic Order', Nigerian Institute of International Affairs, 20-3 Oct., 1977

Langley, K., 'The External Resource Factor in Nigerian Economic Development', *Nigerian Journal of Economic and Social Studies*, vol. 10, no. 2, July, 1968

Senghor, L., *On African Socialism*, Pall Mall Press, London, 1964

Wolf, C. Jr. and Sufrin, S.C., *Capital Formation and Foreign Investment in Underdeveloped Areas*, Syracuse University Press, Syracuse, New York, 1958

2 DEVELOPMENTS IN NIGERIA'S OIL POLICY

When Nigeria became independent in 1960, the government switched over from bilateral political and economic relationships with the United Kingdom to a multilateral policy of political, economic and commercial relationships with the rest of the world. During the colonial period, the UK acted as the middleman in the purchase and sale of Nigeria's raw materials to the rest of the world. When oil was discovered it was added to the list of Nigeria's raw materials and marketed by a British-sponsored oil Company — Shell BP.

The oil industry was one of the industries in which Nigeria embarked on policy changes considering the political, military, economic and strategic importance of oil as a raw material. To begin with, the monopoly of Shell BP had to be broken. When Shell D'arcy, which later was renamed Shell BP, began operations in Nigeria in 1937 the *Colonial Mineral Ordinance* granted the company the entire onshore and offshore oil exploration and prospecting rights. These concessions had to be formally abrogated but this was not achieved until 1969, almost a decade after Nigeria's independence. Before the formal abrogation of the Colonial Mineral Ordinance, Shell BP had already restricted its operations to the Niger Delta area in the South of Nigeria.

1. Petroleum Decree (Act) No. 51 of 1969

Spirited efforts were made in 1969 to amend the Colonial Mineral Ordinance of 1914 in order to strengthen Nigeria's hold on the oil industry, especially in the granting of oil exploration and oil prospecting licences as well as oil-mining leases. With the *Petroleum Decree No. 51* of 1969 further legislation was passed in order to improve Nigeria's influence over, and control of, the oil industry, particularly in the areas of oil refining, distribution and uniform prices for petroleum products. In the area of the oil industry generally, the Petroleum Decree No. 51 of 1969 vests the entire ownership and control of all petroleum found under or upon any Nigerian lands, territorial water or within Nigeria's continental shelf with the Nigerian government or its agencies. The Decree

19

clearly distinguished between *Exploration Licences* which entitle the holder to explore for petroleum, *Prospecting Licences* which entitle the holder to prospect for petroleum and *Mining Leases* which allow the holder to search, win, work, carry away and dispose of petroleum.

Exploration, Prospecting Licences and Mining Leases are to be granted only to Nigerian citizens or companies incorporated in Nigeria. Only the Commissioner (Minister since October, 1979) for Petroleum Resources is entitled by law to grant licences or leases on the payment of prescribed fees. The Commissioner also has the right to revoke any licences or leases if the operators of such licences or leases acted in a manner contrary to Nigeria's interests.

Schedule I of the Decree entitles the holder of an oil exploration licence to prospect but not drill for oil in the area specified in the licence and the licence 'shall not confer any exclusive operational rights to the holder in the area so specified'. The Commissioner reserves the right to grant further licences (exploration and prospecting) and leases to other interested parties in the same area. Oil exploration licences expire automatically on 31 December of each year but can be renewed if the licensee has fulfilled all the obligations demanded by the Decree and applied for a renewal at least three months before the expiry date. The licensee must also show evidence of intensive exploration in the area in which renewal is sought during the period in which the licence was valid.

Oil prospecting licences on the other hand entitle the holder to an exclusive right to prospect and drill for petroleum in the area specified in the licence. The holder of such a licence may carry away and dispose of petroleum on fulfilling certain obligations such as the payment of fees and petroleum tax or other obligations imposed by the Commissioner. The duration of an oil prospecting licence shall not exceed five years and shall be determined by the Commissioner.

An oil mining lease combines exploration, prospecting and the right to mine crude oil for a period not exceeding 20 years in the first instance and is renewable. An oil mining lease can only be granted to Nigerian citizens or any incorporated company which has successfully carried out oil exploration and prospecting and discovered oil in commercial quantities. Oil in commercial quantities was defined as meaning the production of at least

10,000 barrels of crude oil per day in the licensed area. An oil mining lease is also exclusive to the holder within the leased area and entitles the holder to explore, to prospect and 'to win, ... store, carry away, transport, export or otherwise treat petroleum discovered in or under the leased area'. The Lessee must relinquish one-half of the area leased to him after ten years. This is to ensure that the Lessee does not keep a lease indefinitely without carrying out intensive oil production activities in the area leased to him. The Lessee must apply for a renewal within a period of not less than twelve months from the expiry date of the lease. The renewal may only be granted if the Commissioner is satisfied that the Lessee had fulfilled all his obligations including the payment of prescribed fees and royalties.

Licences and leases are not transferrable without the expressed permission of the Commissioner, that is after the Commissioner has satisfied himself that the proposed assignee can perform. The holder of a licence or lease reserves the right to terminate his licence or lease, but he must give three months notice of his intention in writing. The Commissioner himself also reserves the right to revoke any licence or lease if the operation of such licences or leases is contrary to the interests of the Federal Republic of Nigeria or if the holder of such licences or leases failed in their obligations.

The Petroleum Decree No. 51 of 1969 prescribes for the appointment of a Chief Petroleum Engineer to be solely responsible to the Federal Government of Nigeria. The functions of the Petroleum Engineer include the writing of annual reports to the Federal Government on the operations of the licensees and lessees in the areas in which they were granted concessions. The Chief Petroleum Engineer inspects oil installations to ensure that they performed in accordance with the objectives on which the concession was based. Where the licensee or the lessee is operating contrary to the agreement or where operations are considered dangerous to civilisation, the Chief Petroleum Engineer has the right and the authority to suspend such operations with the knowledge of the Commissioner for Mines and Power. The Chief Petroleum Engineer can also arrest or cause to be arrested anyone infringing the decrees relating to oil production and evacuation.

As a result of Nigeria's new oil policies a number of companies began to apply for *Oil Prospecting Licences* (OPL) which allowed a company to prospect and drill for oil as opposed to *Oil Exploration*

Licences (OEL) which allowed a company to prospect, and not drill, for oil. The new prospecting policy attracted a number of foreign oil companies. The major oil companies which later joined Shell BP are American Overseas Petroleum (which later became known as Texaco), Mobil, Tennessee Nigeria Incorporated now called Tenneco, Gulf, Nigerian Agip Oil Company, Safrap now called ELF and Esso West Africa. More oil companies have appeared since the 1960s on the Nigerian oil scene. They are Pan Ocean, Ashland and Phillips. These oil companies are engaged in Seismic/Geophysical activities, drilling, oil production and, to an extent, gas production. They also export crude oil. The largest of them all is still Shell in terms of Seismic activities, drilling of exploration wells, appraisal/development wells, crude oil and gas production and crude oil exports. In the autumn of 1979 the Nigerian government acquired the British Petroleum shares of Shell BP. It became administered by the (NNPC) Nigeria National Petroleum Company. The activities of the oil companies will be examined in Chapter four.

2. Nigerian Equity Participation in the Oil Industry

The new Nigerian oil policy of participation in equity capital began with the agreement reached between the Nigerian Agip Oil Company (NAOC), a subsidiary of the Italian Oil Company, ENI. The company was incorporated in Nigeria in 1962. In the agreement between the Nigerian government and NAOC there was a provision in the concession agreement which allowed the Nigerian government an option to participate in the equity of the company by thirty-three and one-third per cent ($33\frac{1}{3}$ per cent). This was the first ever equity participation by the Nigerian government in the oil business and it paved the way for similar arrangements with other oil companies, especially in the 1970s. According to the agreement reached with NAOC, the company alone invested its own funds in seismic and geophysical activities, drilling and oil production. Nigeria had the option to participate in an equity interest if the company struck oil in commercial quantities. The agreement with NAOC minimised investment risks for the Nigerian government since its equity interest could only be paid when there was abundant evidence that oil was available in commercial quantities.

In the 1960s Nigeria was ill-experienced and ill-equipped for the oil business. It lacked the technical know-how, equipment and funds to participate fully in the oil industry. Its approach to oil policy was therefore a very cautious one to avoid scaring away oil investors in the Nigerian economy. The terms of the Oil Prospecting Licences already imposed certain obligations which the Colonial Mineral Oil Ordinance of 1914 deliberately omitted. The oil prospecting licences agreement made it mandatory for companies granted oil prospecting concessions to develop indigenous manpower, to provide certain infrastructure and utilities in the areas of operation, to pay rents and royalties to the Federal Government according to the terms of agreement.

It was in the 1970s that Nigeria took some bolder steps towards greater participation in the oil industry. For the first time it exercised its option to acquire a $33\frac{1}{3}$ per cent equity interest in NAOC when the company discovered oil in commercial quantities in 1970. The acquisition took place on 1 April 1971. On the same date the Federal Government acquired 35 per cent equity interest in Safrap (ELF) to punish the company for the political and military support allegedly given to Biafra during the Nigeria/Biafra war (1967-70). The equity interest acquisition in Safrap exceeded that of NAOC by $1\frac{2}{3}$ per cent. The punitive element in the acquisition of part of Safrap's equity interest lies in the fact that the acquisition was not as a result of Nigeria exercising an agreed option as it was in the case of NAOC. Nigeria's admission into OPEC in July 1971 encouraged a more aggressive oil policy along the lines of other OPEC members. A major objective which motivated the forming of OPEC was to form a united front against the industrialised countries, the major consumers of oil and who directly or indirectly and in conjunction with their oil companies dictated the prices to be paid for various grades of oil. Until OPEC was formed, these were ridiculously low. OPEC as a body therefore strived to ensure that her members actively participated in the oil operations of those companies granted concessions to prospect for oil in the member countries. It also regulated the production quotas of member countries in order to achieve a uniform and attractive price in the world oil market. Uncontrolled production was bound to increase the world supply of oil over and above the world demand for it, a situation which would obviously push down the price of oil on the international market and jeopardise the financial interests of member countries.

As far back as June, 1968 OPEC had taken the bull by the

horns when resolution XVI.90 was passed which obligated its members to deliberately acquire equity interests in the oil industries of their respective countries and to participate actively in all oil operations. A timetable was set up and member countries were expected to have acquired 51 per cent equity participation in their oil industries by the year 1982, which was set as the deadline. When Nigeria joined OPEC in July, 1971, it took note of the resolution but preferred a gradualistic approach. It acquired 35 per cent equity interest in the three major companies which at that time had begun to produce oil in commercial quantities The companies were Shell BP, Gulf and Mobil. With the acquisition of a 35 per cent equity interest in the three companies a partnership situation developed between the Nigerian government and the oil companies. Unlike the agreement with NAOC, Nigeria became an active participant in Shell BP, Gulf and Mobil, paid in her own funds and took the risk by investing directly. In return, Nigeria participated in the sharing of crude oil *in specie*, which Nigeria was free to sell as the case might be. Equity interest payments in the oil companies were on the basis of the up-dated book value of company assets. This was the OPEC formula for member countries seeking participation in the oil businesses of their respective countries.

From participation based on up-dated book value as was the case in 1971, Nigeria switched over to participation based on net-book value as from 1974, a result of Libya's nationalisation of some oil companies and the successful negotiation to pay compensation based on net-book value. Table 2.1 shows the various joint venture participation interests of the Federal Government in the oil companies and the percentage participations as well as the dates of participation.

3. Further Attempts to Improve the Joint Oil Venture Relationship with the Oil Companies

In an attempt to improve the joint venture relationships between the Federal Government of Nigeria and foreign oil companies, various forms of contracts such as the Production Sharing Contract (PSC) and the Risk Service Contract (RSC) were devised.

Table 2.1: Joint Venture Participation Interests of the Nigerian Government in the Exploratory and Exploitation Sector of the Oil Industry

Company	Participation (%)	Date Acquired
ELF	35	1 April 1971
	55	1 April 1974
	60	1 July 1979
AGIP/PHILLIPS	$33\frac{1}{3}$[a]	1 April 1971
	55	1 April 1974
	60	1 July 1979
SHELL BP	35	1 April 1973
	55	1 April 1974
	60	1 July 1979
	80	1 August 1979
GULF	35	1 April 1973
	55	1 April 1974
	60	1 July 1979
MOBIL	35	1 April 1973
	55	1 April 1974
	60	1 July 1979
TEXACO	55	1 May 1975
	60	1 July 1979
PAN OCEAN	55	1 January 1978
	60	1 July 1979
ASHLAND[b]	n.a.	June 1973

Notes: a. Equity participation.
b. NNPC/Ashland arrangement is a production-sharing agreement.

Source: *NAPETCOR*, quarterly magazine of the Nigerian National Petroleum Corporation, vol. 2, no. 1, January-March, 1981.

(a) Production Sharing Contract (PSC)

This form of contract agreement was devised to improve the traditional joint venture arrangements between Nigeria and foreign oil companies. Because of her inadequacy in terms of technological know-how, technological and executive manpower and her limited finances for a frontal approach to economic development, Nigeria had little or no option but to go into this form of contract which has its shortcomings. It was already difficult, finding enough funds for the massive programmes in transportation, power supply, agricultural and industrial developments contained in Nigeria's *Fifteen Years Development Plan.* The strains of the war were still very apparent and Nigeria's foreign reserves were virtually depleted during the war years (June, 1967 to January, 1970). Nigeria therefore lacked the capacity to commit scarce funds to a very capital intensive industry such as the oil industry. Moreover, the Iron and Steel Mill Industry which had been on the drawing board since the early part of the 1960s had not been properly motivated, partly because of the locational politics of the industry and the type of technology to be used, but mainly because of the inadequacy of funding and manpower.

In the light of the above, the Federal Government had to be contented with contracts in which the benefits only marginally outweighed the costs to the nation. The Production Sharing Contract was designed to accommodate new oil companies in an already existing concession originally owned by Shell BP but later transferred to Nigeria's own oil company, without altering the legal status of the existing company

A Production Sharing Contract allows partners to contribute funds for capital and operational activities in an agreed proportion and to share crude oil *in specie* in the proportion of their equity interests. The foreign oil company therefore becomes a contractor and is only entitled to a percentage of the total crude oil production which will enable it to recover a greater part of its investments. In addition, the contractor was also allowed to participate in the sharing of the balance of crude oil after expenses such as royalties and taxes had been deducted. The Production Sharing Contract is said to have a number of shortcomings. For example, the foreign oil company (contractor) may wish to limit its exploratory activities once it strikes oil in commercial quantities since only a small fraction of crude oil will be shared out to it for the purpose of investment recovery each time a new discovery is made. It may also decide to concentrate on crude oil production in an existing oil field where no further exploratory investments are required. The PSC system kills incentives in an economy in which oil is the main income earner as it has been in Nigeria since the 1970s. A contractor may by the PSC system reap a large profit from little investment if a large oil field with a huge reserve of crude oil is discovered which can be tapped for many years. Most investment costs in the oil industry are incurred at the exploratory stage.

The PSC agreement was first signed with the Ashland Oil

Company in 1973. According to the contractual agreement between Nigeria and the Ashland Oil Company, the company provided funds for exploration, development and oil production on behalf of the Nigerian government. In the event of crude oil discovery, 40 per cent of crude is set aside for the amortisation of the company's investments and for the payment of royalties while 55 per cent is put aside for the purpose of settling Petroleum Profit Tax (PPT). The balance of whatever remained was shared *in specie* between the Federal Government and the Ashland Company in the ratio of 65:35 respectively for crude oil production up to 50,000 barrels per day. For all production exceeding 50,000 barrels per day the ratio varied to 70:30.

(b) Risk Service Contract (RSC)

The Risk Service Contract is a more specific form of contract than the Production Sharing Contract and it offers more concrete advantages than those of the PSC. The RSC makes it mandatory for the foreign oil company (contractor) to undertake all forms of investment relating to exploration, development and oil production activities. Unlike the PSC which embraces a number of oil prospecting leases, the RSC limits the contractor to one contract area and the contract period was set at between two to five years with the contract terminating at the ceiling year as specified in the contract. When oil is not discovered in commercial quantities, the contract terminates. Again unlike the PSC the contractor has no title to crude oil but he can demand that his investment be repaid and that his remuneration be paid in crude oil. If oil is discovered in commercial quantities the contractor can exercise the option to purchase specified quantities of crude oil generated in the area defined in the service contract. The RSC has some advantages over the PSC in that it accelerates oil exploration in the contract area and offers the contractor an equitable return on his investment should oil be discovered in commercial quantities. It also guarantees that the contractor continues to benefit from crude oil for an indefinite perod, far beyond the ceiling year period specified in the contract agreement. More than eleven RSC agreements have been signed between the NNPC and Agip Africa, Elf and Nigus Petroleum. The agreements include both offshore and onshore contracts. The RSC agreements are yielding some dividends as the oil companies have already struck oil within a record time.

References and Additional Reading

Adams, G.A., 'Joint Ventures in Nigerian Oil Industry — What are they?', in
    NAPETCOR, Lagos, vol. 2, no. 1, Jan.–March 1981
Asiodu, P.C., *Nigerians and Their Oil Industry*, Ministry of Mines and Power,
    Lagos, 1972
Eno J. Usoro, 'Oil Companies and Recent Nigerian Petroleum Oil Policies', in *The
    Nigerian Journal of Economic and Social Studies*, Nov. 1972
Holmes, P.F., *Statement of General Business Principles*, Shell Petroleum
    Development Company Nig. Ltd., Dec. 1979
'Joint Venture in the Nigerian Economy' in *Sunday Statesman*, Nigeria, 16 May
    1982
NNPC, *Progress of Public Sector Participation in the Nigerian Oil Industry*,
    NNPC, Lagos, 1978
Shell BP, *The Story of Shell BP*, Irede Printers, Isolo Road, Mushin, Lagos, 1974

3 FORMATION OF NIGERIA'S OWN OIL COMPANY

With the ending of the Nigeria/Biafra war, there was a general stock-taking of the Nigerian economy. Questions were asked about the future of the Nigerian economy and in particular the Nigerian oil industry. Doubts were expressed as to the possible future contributions of foreign oil companies to the development of the Nigerian economy. The increasing role of oil in international politics and the use of oil as an instrument for international diplomacy became recognised. Moreover it was widely believed in Nigerian circles that the war between Nigeria and the defunct Biafra could not have lasted so long had a French oil company not been involved in the Biafran region. Nigeria began gradually to appreciate that it possessed an important instrument which could be wielded to achieve a number of international policy objectives. The ability of Nigeria to use oil to achieve international objectives depended largely upon her effective control of the oil industry. Consequently Nigeria's oil policy was reassessed. New policies defined the new roles the Federal Government was expected to play in an industry which had become Nigeria's major income earner, and which was expected to form the base for Nigeria's industrial takeoff and of technological transfer.

The operating oil companies in Nigeria were reassessed in terms of their contributions to the transfer of technology and to the general economic and social developments of the country. The oil companies were found very much wanting in these respects. They were no less different from other multinationals which had gained notoriety in many parts of the world as organisations which took away as much as possible from poor countries where they operate leaving little or nothing in return.

The foreign oil companies operating in Nigeria had no programme to indigenise their operations or to transfer oil technology to Nigerians. There were few Nigerians employed in professional, technical and supervisory positions, most were employed on a contract basis and were not accorded the same conditions of service as their foreign counterparts. There were allegations of discriminatory, even humiliating treatment of Nigerian members of staff of the oil companies. In almost all cases foreign oil companies preferred the use of foreign consultants in the planning and designing of oil equipment and facilities. All preproduction works such as data processing of seismic records were carried on at overseas centres. No attempts were made by the oil companies to install facilities in Nigeria and no laboratories for the analysis of crude oil, gas and other related by-products were established in Nigeria. The oil companies imported virtually all equipment and materials such as steel pipes, chemicals, drilling mud and cements, and there were no established facilities for producing some of these materials in Nigeria. The oil industry ought to have a number of forward and backward linkage effects in any oil economy, but these effects were hardly felt in the case of Nigeria. The view became popular that the only way to generate the desired economic impact of the oil industry was through government regulations of the terms under which the oil companies operate in Nigeria. Obviously the most reasonable thing to do in these circumstances was to establish Nigeria's own oil company which would market the Federal Government's share of crude oil direct to international oil consumers and not through intermediaries as had hitherto been the case.

1. Nigerian National Oil Corporation (NNOC)

Decree No. 18 of 1971 established the Nigerian National Oil Corporation in 1971, the year Nigeria joined OPEC, and in response to OPEC resolution No. XVI.90 of 1968 which obligated members to acquire 51 per cent of the equity interests of foreign oil companies operating in their countries and to participate actively in all aspects of oil operations. NNOC was also to recruit and train indigenous manpower which Nigeria was expected to contribute in joint venture schemes with foreign oil companies. The foreign oil companies themselves had already been directed by the *Petroleum Regulations* of 1969 to indigenise their manpower up to 70 per cent within seven years of operations and to gradually indigenise the remaining manpower in the shortest possible time. The Nigerian National Oil Company was granted oil leases over a large area and was allowed to take over the concessions withdrawn from foreign companies in the course of time as new agreements on job ventures continued to be negotiated with foreign companies. NNOC was expected to train an adequate number of engineers, geologists and managers of various cadres for its own use, to hire foreign contractors to work for it on agreed payment terms which may be cash or oil *in specie.* This marked the beginning of the various forms of sharing agreement discussed in the preceding chapter.

NNOC was also expected to encourage indigenous private participation in such services as the supply of materials, catering, road construction to the oil fields and provision of lorries and tippers for evacuation purposes. It was expected to indigenise areas such as seismic and drilling operations in the shortest practicable time. NNOC was also expected to manage the petroleum refineries which had been set up or were expected to be set up, to participate actively in the orderly marketing of petroleum products in the country and to ensure that uniform prices obtained in the petroleum products market of Nigeria, irrespective of the distance of the market from the refinery. NNOC was therefore to review the distribution and marketing policies of petroleum products which hitherto had been under the control of a few oil and gas marketing companies. These companies were foreign and duplicated overhead costs which were eventually transferred to Nigerian consumers. In the area of transportation NNOC was to develop a National Tanker Fleet to evacuate crude oil from Nigerian terminals to overseas markets. NNOC was also to investigate the possibilities of starting allied oil industries such as petrochemicals and fertiliser projects in order to satisfy Nigeria's domestic demand and for export purposes in the event of expansion.

The Nigerian National Oil Corporation was also entrusted with the construction and laying of pipes for the carriage or conveyance of resources such as crude oil, natural gas or any other liquid; to construct, equip and maintain tank farms and other facilities, and to perform other functions which the organisation might be called upon to perform from time to time.

The law establishing the corporation entitled it to sue and be sued as a corporate entity; to hold and manage movable and immovable assets for the corporation; to purchase, acquire or take over an asset, or part of an asset, business, property, liability of any company, firm or individual in the course of carrying out its legitimate operations. NNOC could enter into contracts or partnerships with any other company, firm or individual in the course of carrying out these duties. The corporation was however not allowed by the law establishing it to borrow money or to dispose of any of the corporation's assets without the specific approval of the Commissioner. Surplus funds of the corporation could only be disposed of on the directions of the Commissioner and subject to the approval of the Federal Executive Council. The corporation invested its surplus funds as directed by the Federal Executive Council and was expected to maintain a general reserve and to prepare and submit an annual report to the Commissioner not later than three months after the end of each financial year.

In carrying out its duties the Nigerian National Oil Corporation was expected to adhere to the terms of the decree establishing it and to seek clearance from the Federal Executive Council through the Commissioner before embarking on any other activities not specified in Decree No. 18. This Decree further provided for the appointment of a general manager and secretary to the corporation. The appointment of the general manager (the chief executive) by the Federal Executive Council was on the recommendation of the Commissioner for Mines and Power. Members of the Board were also appointed on the recommendation of the Commissioner although the Decree was silent on how the Board members were to be appointed. The Board itself was responsible for the appointment of the secretary to the corporation whose duty included the keeping of the corporation's records and the conducting of correspondence and other duties which the Board from time to time directed the secretary to perform. The Decree did not specify the functions of the secretary.

The NNOC Board of Directors comprised the Permanent Secretary to the Ministry of Mines and Power who was also the Chairman of the Board; Permanent Secretaries or the representatives of the Ministries of Finance, and Economic Development and Planning; the Director of Petroleum Resources in the Ministry of Mines and Power; the General Manager of NNOC and three other persons who in the view of the Commissioner for Mines and Power possessed the specialised knowledge, experience and capacity to contribute meaningfully in the deliberations of the Board.

NNOC was not itself an Operating Company but a Holding Company which provided policy guidelines for its subsidiaries and implemented government decisions and intentions. Figure 3.1 shows the organisational structure of the NNOC, which had three major divisions:

(1) Legal and Economic Division
(2) Finance, Accounts and Economics Division
(3) Administration Division (Staffing Administration, Training, Information, and Employee and Industrial Relations).

Figure 3.1: The Structure of the Nigerian National Oil Corporation

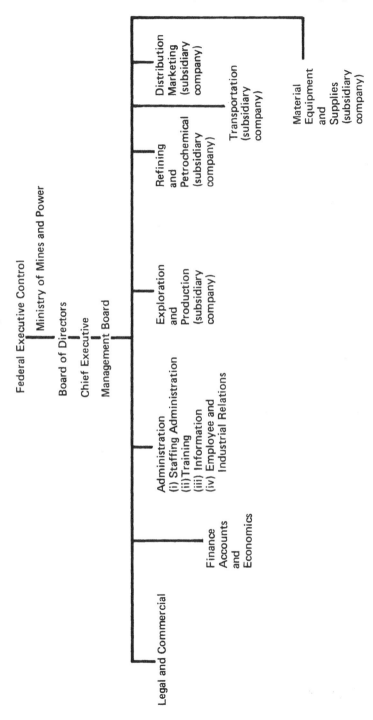

The subsidiary companies of the NNOC were as follows:

(1) Exploration and Production
(2) Refining and Petro Chemical
(3) Transportation
(4) Distribution and Marketing
(5) Material Equipment and Supplies.

With a few exceptions NNOC operated like any other holding company, although it was not required to relinquish a half of the area leased to it after ten years and its prospecting and mining licences were not limited to 5 and 20 years respectively as was the case with foreign oil companies. In its operations NNOC was bound in every respect, as were the foreign oil companies, by the Petroleum Decree of 1969 (with the exception of paragraph 12 of Schedule I of the Petroleum Decree and the Oil Pipelines Act of 1965). Like any other company its accounts were audited yearly and an Audit Report forwarded to the Board. The Auditor of NNOC was appointed with the approval of the Commissioner.

2. Nigerian National Petroleum Corporation (NNPC)

With the increased participation of Nigeria in the oil industry it became imperative to establish a new oil company endowed with wider powers and freed from some of the restrictions imposed on NNOC. Accordingly the Nigerian National Petroleum Corporation (NNPC) was established by Decree No. 33 of 1 April 1977. The Nigerian National Petroleum Corporation took over the assets and liabilities of NNOC. Some of the functions of the divisions in the Ministry of Mines and Power were added to the functions NNPC inherited from NNOC. In addition to the general functions of NNOC which NNPC inherited, NNPC was entrusted with the duties of conducting researches relating to the petroleum industry and the results of such researches were to be put into practical use. The supervision of all oil contract agreements entered into by the Federal Government fell on NNPC.

The new corporation also inherited all the powers of NNOC, for example, to sue and be sued; to hold and manage movable and immovable property; to purchase or enter into contracts or partnership agreements with individuals or companies, and to train managerial, technical and other staff required for its operations.

Unlike the defunct NNOC which had powers to award contracts of up to ₦100,000, only NNPC had powers to award contracts to the value of ₦5 million. All contracts exceeding ₦5 million were to be referred to the Federal Executive Council. While NNOC was not allowed to borrow without the approval of the Federal Executive Council, NNPC had borrowing powers but the limit of borrowing was specified by the Federal Executive Council, and this is revised from time to time. However, any borrowing in currency other than the Naira and which has to be repaid over a long period must have the prior approval of the Federal Executive Council. The accounts of the corporation are also subject to annual auditing and an Annual Report is expected to be prepared every year on the activities of NNPC. Surplus funds of the corporation can only be invested or disposed of as directed by the Federal Executive Council.

NNPC is subject to all laws and decrees in connection with the Oil Industry. The Board had a similar composition to that of the defunct NNOC with the exception that the Federal Commissioner for Petroleum became the Chairman of the Board instead of a Permanent Secretary of the Ministry. Since the civilian administration began in October, 1979, an outsider has been the chairman of the Board of NNPC.

A new department of Petroleum Inspectorate was approved for NNPC by Decree No. 33 and a Chief Executive appointed. The Petroleum Inspectorate has been delegated the following functions by the Federal Commissioner for Petroleum without any prejudice to the Oil Pipelines Act of 1965 or the Petroleum Decree of 1969. The delegated functions are as follows:

(1) To issue licences for activities connected with petroleum exploration and exploitation, crude oil refining, storage, marketing, transportation and distribution of petroleum products. (These functions were originally carried out by the subsidiaries of NNPC.)

(2) To act as the agent for the enforcement of the provisions of the Oil Pipelines Act and the Petroleum Decree.

(3) To carry out any other functions which the Commissioner for Petroleum may assign the Inspectorate from time to time.

The Chief Executive of the Petroleum Inspectorate Department was freed from any control of the NNPC Board or of any other body.

He was directly responsible to the Federal Commissioner for Petroleum.

NNPC oversees government interests in joint oil ventures with foreign partners in which the government is the silent partner, while the foreign partners who bring with them the necessary funds, and the technological know-how, are the main operators. NNPC is the watchdog of the government and ensures that government interests are fully protected without prejudice to the rights of foreign operators. NNPC liaises with foreign partners in oil programming; budgeting matters, field visits and in technical matters.

At the disposal of NNPC are various cadres of professionals such as lawyers, economists, accountants, geologists, geophysicists and engineers of various skills for the purposes of effective liaison with foreign oil partners. NNPC has a permanent Joint Venture Co-ordinating Committee in the Joint Venture Department of the Exploration and Exploitation Division. The Joint Venture Committee co-ordinates the activities of the oil companies and manages the various joint venture contracts with the oil companies.

3. The Nigerian Crude Oil Scandal

The Nigerian National Petroleum Company was formed in 1977, as a result of the merging of the Nigerian National Oil Company and some departments of the Ministry of Mines and Power. Hardly two years after the formation of NNPC, a scandal erupted in the corporation. A national newspaper, *Punch*, alleged in its issue of 19 September 1979 that an oil money totalling ₦2.841 billion was missing from NNPC's account with the Midland Bank of London. The missing money was said to be lodged in the private accounts of a third party oil purchaser of the Nigerian National Petroleum Corporation. NNPC's official denial of the allegation did not stop the rumour spreading. In November, 1979, the issue was raised on the floor of the Senate. The echo of the rumour reverberated once more throughout the length and breadth of the country. On 28 March 1980 the issue was again raised in the House of Representatives. By April, 1980, it had become household gossip and a national scandal. The President of Nigeria, Alhaji Shehu Shagari had to broadcast to the nation on the issue and set up a high-powered Judicial Commission of Inquiry called the *Crude Oil Sales Tribunal* with a Supreme Court Judge as chairman.

The Panel was given terms of reference which included the investigation of the alleged missing oil money of ₦2.841 billion and other activities of NNPC. Numerous memoranda were forwarded from the public to the Panel. The Panel investigated the records of NNPC, visited the oil fields and heard oral evidence. A number of allegations were made ranging from secret oil contracts to the notorious activities of third party oil buyers and the incompatibility of oil production records as given by NNPC and foreign oil companies respectively. The Panel also visited countries such as the United Kingdom and the United States of America and spoke to a number of banks which included the Midland Bank of London, Federal Reserve Bank of New York, Banque National de Paris Limited, London, and the Bank of England. A major allegation made during the sitting of the Tribunal concerned the improper conduct of third party oil buyers who were alleged to have robbed Nigeria of ₦12 billion through clandestine operations. The third party agents relied on commissions based on the quantity of oil sold for NNPC. Although the amount appeared exaggerated there was clearly an element of truth in the allegation. In some cases these third party agents banked the proceeds of sales in their own private accounts instead of paying the proceeds into NNPC's account. By lodging the sums in their private accounts over a long period, benefits were obtained from the high deposit rates of foreign banks. In nearly every case the Internal Revenue did not assess the earnings of such third party agents for the purposes of tax payments. Some agents were known to have refused to pay their debts and no system was set up to recover such debts. Among the debtors of NNPC were Ghana, Togo, a West German firm and an American oil company.

NNPC was accused of inefficiency both in the marketing of crude oil and in the keeping of oil production records. The fall in oil revenue in 1978 was attributed partly to fluctuations in world oil prices but mainly to overstocking of crude oil by NNPC in the (incorrect) anticipation of rising world market prices of oil.

NNPC workers and customs officials were accused of indolence in the performance of their duties with respect to Nigerian oil exports. The oil companies were alleged to have completed oil loading forms relating to the quantity of oil carried away by them which NNPC and customs officials signed without the precaution of crosschecking them. As a witness put it '… when the deepening and loading were completed we would be called upon to endorse the documents'. NNPC and Nigerian customs officials were alleged to have received gratuitous payments from foreign oil companies or their agents and from third party buyers. As the Chairman of the Panel himself remarked '... it is difficult if not impossible to determine the volume of crude oil being taken away from the country. Because of circumstances beyond their control, your men (NNPC) were looking the other way while our oil was being carried away.' Justice Irikefe further remarked that the Nigerian Oil Inspectors the Panel saw during the field tour to the oil terminals were no match for the alien oil men in intelligence, experience and technical skills. It was also alleged that the equipment used for calculating the volume of crude oil loaded into oil tankers was brought into the country by foreign oil companies. It was therefore hardly surprising that the records of oil produced and exported from Nigeria as given by NNPC were markedly different from those given by the foreign oil companies themselves.

There were also serious allegations of 'hush-hush' contracts with three oil companies a few days before Shagari's civilian government took over the administration of Nigeria in October, 1979. It was alleged that nine contracts were signed between NNPC and the Nigus Petroleum (Nig.) Ltd., AGIP Africa Ltd. and ELF (Nig.) Ltd. seven days before the civilian administration took office. The three oil companies signed two, four and three contracts with NNPC respectively. The contract termed *Means and Service Contracts* entitled the three companies to explore for oil on behalf of NNPC, while NNPC paid for the exploration activities. It was alleged that between 1976 and May, 1979 a total of 19 contracts were signed. There were also allegations that a company blacklisted for non-performance in an earlier ₦20 million contract, and which had forfeited a ₦250,000 deposit, was awarded a contract worth $30 million to purchase Nigerian crude oil. The blacklisted company lifted four consignments of crude oil from Nigerian oil terminals but paid for only one and absconded. The company in question was named as WILCO Oil Incorporated.

4. The Re-organisation of NNPC

Although the Crude Oil Sales Tribunal in its report submitted on 30 June 1980 described the allegation that oil money worth ₦2.8 billion was missing as the 'Hoax' of all times, the report nevertheless established that NNPC was too large an organisation to be managed efficiently. It recommended strongly the decentralisation of the corporation and the reorganisation of the administration to reflect the policy of decentralisation.

Accordingly, a Presidential Bill was brought to the National Assembly in 1981 for the reorganisation of NNPC to make it a viable and efficient corporation, in view of the domestic impact of the oil industry on the Nigerian economy and the strategic importance of oil in global world politics. The Presidential Bill was passed with some amendments. Apart from a part-time chairman of ministerial rank and a vice-chairman who would also be the chief executive of the corporation, the bill as passed recommended the creation of a Ministry of Petroleum and Energy. The Minister in charge of the new ministry would then be the Chairman of the Board of NNPC. The objective of this amendment was to speed up decisions on oil policy matters as the Minister can table such policy matters directly to the President in Council. The bill as proposed by the President envisaged that all project proposals of NNPC would be forwarded through the Managing Director (also the Vice-Chairman), and through the Federal Minister (also the part-time Chairman) and through the Presidential Adviser on Petroleum to the President in Council. The proposed chanelling procedures of NNPC proposals have been criticised as cumbersome and likely to fall foul of bureaucratic bottlenecks; it was feared that NNPC policy proposals might be muddled up *en route* by bureaucrats ignorant of the underlying assumptions and the rationale behind the formulation of the policy proposals. Again, speed is of the essence in view of the fact that Nigerian oil policy is inextricably tied to the oil policy of OPEC, the responses of international consumers and the policies of other non-OPEC competitors who produce the same grades of oil as does Nigeria. It was also argued that Nigeria's ability to play an active part in OPEC of which it is a member was contingent upon Nigeria's OPEC delegation being led by a Petroleum Minister conversant with oil problems and policy. A Minister of Petroleum and Energy was consistent with arrangements made in other OPEC countries. In the light of the above arguments the bill was passed, so providing for the creation of a Ministry of Petroleum and Energy.

The National Assembly also passed an amendment which created nine subsidiaries of NNPC in order to enhance the efficiency of operations in the oil industry and to encourage specialisation and self-accountability. Even though no evidence could be established about the ₦2.8 billion alleged to be missing, it was evident that NNPC was not well organised. By creating nine subsidiaries in which each subsidiary takes policy decisions and becomes self-accountable, it was hoped that the inefficiency in the accounting system of NNPC would be eliminated.

The following nine subsidiaries were created:

(1) Nigerian Petroleum Exploration and Exploitation Company Limited (NPEEC)
(2) Nigerian Petroleum Refining Company, Kaduna Limited (NPRC, Kaduna, Ltd.)
(3) Nigerian Petroleum Refining Company, Warri Limited (NPRC, Warri, Ltd.)
(4) Nigerian Petroleum Refining Company, Port Harcourt Limited (NPRC, PH., Ltd.)
(5) Nigerian Petroleum Products Pipelines and Depots Company Limited (NPPD Co., Ltd.)
(6) Nigerian Petro Chemicals Company Limited (NPCC, Ltd.)
(7) Nigerian Gas Company Limited (NGC, Ltd.)
(8) Nigerian Petroleum Marine Transportation Company Limited (NPMTC, Ltd.)
(9) Petroleum Research and Engineering Company Limited (PREC, Ltd.).

As can be seen above the refineries were further decentralised in order to create competition between the companies and to limit their areas of operations in order to enhance efficiency. The Nigerian oil territory is so vast that it would be difficult for one company alone to manage the various refineries. The refining sector also controls about 60 per cent of Nigerian oil industry manpower. The decentralisation of the refineries will make for greater efficiency, and enhance the management of the manpower resources in the refinery sector.

The new structure has taken shape only gradually but time will tell whether decentralisation has really achieved its aim of enhanced NNPC efficiency or whether it was merely an exercise in futility.

References and Additional Reading

Amu, L.A.O., 'Opening Address', First Delegates Conference of Pengassan, NNPC Branch, Port Harcourt, Nigeria, February, 1982
'Army Rushed 9 Oil Deals in 2 Days', in the *Punch*, Lagos, Nigeria, 23 June 1980

'Awojobi Runs Into a Hitch at Oil Probe', in the *Daily Times*, Lagos, Nigeria, 31 May 1980

'Blacklisted Company Bagged NNPC ₦20m Contract, Tribune Told', in the *Punch*, Lagos, Nigeria, 24 May 1980

'Hoax of All Times', in *NAPETCOR*, vol. 1, no. 1, Oct.–Dec., 1980

'I Don't Know of Any Missing Oil Money', in the *Daily Times*, Lagos, Nigeria, 2 June 1980

'Irikefe Drops a Bombshell', in the *Daily Times*, Lagos, Nigeria, 24 May 1980

'I've No Facts on ₦2.8b, Says Saraki', in the *Daily Times*, Lagos, Nigeria, 30 May 1980

Marinho, F.R.A., 'The Objectives of the NNPC Today and Tomorrow', An Address to NUPENG, Feb., 1980

'New Order at the NNPC', in the *Daily Times*, Lagos, Nigeria, 31 Aug. 1981

'NNPC Man Denies UK Deposit', in the *Punch*, Lagos, Nigeria, 2 June 1980

'NNPC Men Accused of Playing Crude Oil Ball', in the *Daily Times*, Lagos, Nigeria, 7 June 1980

'No Trace of ₦2.8b in London', in the *Daily Times*, Lagos, Nigeria, 5 June 1980

'Obasanjo Not for Oil Probe', in the *Daily Times*, Lagos, Nigeria, 6 June 1980

'Obasanjo, Buhari Dictated Oil Contract', in the *Punch*, Lagos, Nigeria, 2 June 1980

'Oil Probe Told of Daily Production', in the *Daily Times*, Lagos, Nigeria, 4 June 1980

'One Man Controlled the NNPC', in the *Daily Times*, Lagos, Nigeria, 24 May 1980

'Research and Development in NNPC' in *NAPETCOR*, Quarterly Magazine of the Nigerian Petroleum Corporation, vol. 2, no. 2, April–June, 1981

'Senate Cuts NNPC Vote', in the *Daily Times*, Lagos, Nigeria, 11 June 1980

'Third Party Oil Buyers Robbed Nigeria of ₦12b', in the *Daily Times*, Lagos, Nigeria, 29 May 1980

4 THE GROWTH OF THE NIGERIAN PETROLEUM AND ALLIED ENERGY INDUSTRIES

The first attempt to prospect and develop the oil industry in Nigeria can be traced to the year 1908 when a German company, the Nigerian Bitumen Company, began to explore the entire coast of Nigeria for bitumen. The exploration started along the coastal region stretching from Okitipupa to Lagos. At the time the German company was prospecting for bitumen, Nigeria was not firmly a British colony.

With the amalgamation of Northern and Southern Nigeria in 1914 and the outbreak of World War I in 1914 and the subsequent loss of German colonies in Africa such as Cameroon, Togo, Tanganyika and South West Africa (Namibia) in 1918, the German colonial authorities were not only forced out of Africa but most of their commercial interests also folded up. The Nigerian Bitumen Company was one of them. No other attempt was made to prospect for oil in Nigeria partly because of the world recession between 1918 and 1925 and the world depression between 1929 to about 1935. The gloomy world economic picture made it impossible for many European companies to operate outside their own native lands.

With the improvement in the world economic situation and shortly before the outbreak of World War II another company ventured to prospect for oil in Nigeria. It was Shell D'arcy, which in 1937 began to search for oil. Its base was the then provincial capital Owerri, now the capital of Imo State of Nigeria. Shell D'arcy was licensed to search for oil throughout the country but it limited its operations within an area measuring 4,000 square miles or 10,360 square kilometres. It operated mostly in the swampy areas of the Niger Delta. The efforts of Shell D'arcy were halted with the outbreak of World War II. At the end of the war the company resumed operation in 1946. It was the only company licensed by the British to prospect for oil in Nigeria and for a long time it operated under the colonial *Mineral Oil Ordinance No. 17* of 1914 which was amended in 1925 and 1950. The Colonial Ordinance granted prospecting licences only to companies which were registered in the UK, or its protectorates, and such companies were to be manned by principal officers of UK origin or British subjects approved by the British government.

When Shell D'arcy resumed operation in 1946 it formed a partnership with British Petroleum and a new company called the Shell BP Petroleum Company of Nigeria Limited was formed. The new company was formed on the basis of equal partnership between the Royal Dutch Company of the Shell Group of Companies and the British Petroleum Group. Shell BP replaced Shell D'arcy company.

1. The First Oil Strike

After many years of oil prospecting, heavy investment and almost near frustration, Shell BP struck the first oil. The first exploration well was drilled in 1951 at a village called Ihuo about 16 kilometres to the north east of Owerri. The well, which was 3,422 metres deep, yielded no oil but the prospects of discovering oil in commercial quantity became evident. In 1953 another exploratory well, Akata-1 was sunk and crude oil was found but not in commercial quantity. Although the oil discovery was not in commercial quantity that oil had been found at all became a source of encouragement to Shell BP.

In 1956, the operation was moved to the south of Owerri and in 1956 oil was found for the first time in commercial quantity at Olobiri in the riverine area of Nigeria. In the same year another well at Afam in the same riverine region yielded oil in commercial quantity.

With the discovery of oil in commercial quantities in the riverine area, Shell BP moved its operational headquarters to Port Harcourt, a sea port, now the capital of Rivers State of Nigeria. The movement of the oil base to Port Harcourt became necessary because Port Harcourt possessed the necessary infrastructure required for the oil industry, such as a port where tankers loading crude oil could berth and where heavy oil-drilling equipment could be off-loaded. Port Harcourt also possessed an airport and a telecommunications link with Lagos. At Shell BP's new headquarters at Port Harcourt a housing estate, with various utilities such as electricity and water, was established for the workers; workshops and technical schools were established as well as storage facilities.

The major problem encountered in 1956 when oil was found in commercial quantities at Afam and Olobiri was that of evacuation. It was not possible to evacuate any crude oil until 1958 because of the absence of pipelines and because of poor port facilities. In order to evacuate the crude oil, pipelines were constructed, for the first time, between the oil wells and Port Harcourt harbour. In February, 1958 history was made when the first Nigerian crude oil was pumped into a vessel called *Hemifusus.* By 1958, however, only 4,000 barrels per day were being produced.

With the discovery of oil in Olobiri and Afam, Shell BP intensified its search for oil in the riverine areas. Between 1958 and 1959 more oil wells were discovered at Ebubu and Bomu in the riverine areas and at Ughelli in the then Mid-Western Region of Nigeria now called Bendel State. As the oil prospects brightened, Shell BP built two oil terminals at Bonny and Forcados for the purpose of crude oil excavation for the Eastern and Western States respectively. The shallowness of the Bonny bar made it difficult for even small tankers to load crude oil at the terminal. The dredging of the bar became imperative and this was done between 1959 and 1961 in co-operation with the Nigerian Ports Authority. When the dredging was completed, the Bonny bar had a new depth of 37ft or 11.3 metres. The oil terminal at Bonny had four tanks with a total storage capacity of 300,000 barrels of crude oil. Since then more tanks have been completed and each terminal now has a capacity of over 900,000 barrels a day; each terminal also has an offshore loading facility (two single buoy moorings) located at a distance of 25 kilometres to enable tankers of up to 320,000 tons dead weight to be loaded. The Bonny terminal can load up to 90,000 tons dead weight, one result of the dredging of the bar. Shell BP has also constructed pipelines to link the oil wells in Bendel State to the Forcados terminal. About 5,000 kilometres of pipelines have been constructed to connect over 80 oil-producing fields to the terminals at Bonny and Forcados. The seven main trunk lines are: Trans Niger, Trans Forcados, Soku-Bonny, Otumara-Forcados, South Forcados, the Alakiri-Bonny and the Eastern Central trunk lines. The Forcados terminal was completed in 1979 after the civil war.

2. Production of Crude Oil

Thirteen oil companies operate in Nigeria. Some have been granted licences for oil exploration or prospecting. Others have been granted oil mining leases. The conditions for granting oil licences and leases have already been discussed. The oil companies which have benefited from one or more of the various forms of licences or oil mining leases in Nigeria are the following:

(1) Nigerian National Petroleum Corporation (NNPC);
(2) Shell Petroleum Development Company of Nigeria Limited;
(3) Gulf Oil Company (Nig.) Limited;
(4) Mobil Oil Company (Nig.) Limited;
(5) Nigeria Agip Oil Company Limited;
(6) Elf (Nigeria) Limited;
(7) Texaco Overseas Petroleum Company;
(8) Pan Ocean (Nig.) Limited;
(9) Ashland Oil Company (Nig.) Limited;
(10) Phillips Oil Company (Nig.) Limited;
(11) Tenneco Oil Company (Nig.) Limited;
(12) Niger Oil Resource Limited; and
(13) Japan Petroleum Co. (Nig.) Limited.

These companies are involved in the production of crude oil and gases and also in the sale of crude oil. In addition to the above-mentioned activities NNPC, the holding company of the Federal Government of Nigeria, is also involved in oil refining and in the production of allied petroleum products. Although crude oil production in commercial quantities began in earnest in 1958, it was only in the second half of the 1960s that crude oil production became really

Table 4.1: Nigeria's Crude Oil Production Statistics, 1958–82

Year	Production (barrels)	Year	Production (barrels)
1958	1,876,062	1971	558,678,882
1959	4,095,611	1972	643,206,685
1960	6,367,187	1973	750,593,415
1961	16,801,896	1974	823,317,838
1962	24,623,691	1975	651,506,761
1963	27,913,479	1976	758,058,380
1964	43,996,895	1977	766,053,944
1965	99,353,794	1978	692,269,121
1966	152,428,168	1979	842,474,109
1967	116,553,292	1980	754,620,497
1968	51,907,304	1981	381,394,806[a]
1969	197,204,486	1982	474,500,000[a]
1970	395,835,689		

Note: a. Estimates.

Source: Petroleum Inspectorate Annual Report (various issues) and CBN, *Annual Report and Statement of Accounts*, December, 1980.

intensified. Table 4.1 shows the statistics of crude oil production in Nigeria. Since 1970 when Nigeria joined OPEC, Nigeria's crude oil production has been regulated in accordance with the quota allocated to it by OPEC.

There has been a dramatic decline in Nigeria's daily average production rate of crude oil. Instead of an average of 2.2 million barrels a day, Nigeria's average production rate declined by more than half. By March, 1982, the daily average production of Nigeria's crude oil stood at about 950,000 barrels a day. This dramatic decline has been attributed to the world oil glut. OPEC members have been compelled to lower the daily average production quota in order not to precipitate a fall in the world prices of crude oil.

The conservation energy measures taken by the industrialised economies, and the stockpiling of crude oil by consumers for fear that prices might rise, further contributed to the oil glut which has dangerously threatened OPEC's posted prices for oil. Other factors contributing to the present oil glut are the reduction in world oil prices of non-OPEC members and the increase in production of the British National Oil Corporation. The reduction in the price of a barrel of North Sea oil by the British National Oil Corporation affected Nigeria's sales and oil production levels very adversely. While Nigerian oil sold at 35.5 US dollars, the British National Oil Corporation's oil which was of the same quality as that of Nigeria sold between 28 and 30 US dollars. Because Nigerian oil was no longer competitive in international oil markets, foreign oil companies were no longer willing to lift Nigeria's oil. They slowed down their production of oil as it was unreasonable to buy high and sell low.

3. Refined Oil and Associated Products

Only about 16 per cent of Nigeria's oil production is consumed locally. Table 4.2 shows the total annual production and total annual exports The difference between the two indicate the quantity of crude oil refined in Nigeria for domestic use. There are three refineries in Nigeria: Port Harcourt refinery, the oldest of them all; the Warri refinery and the most sophisticated of them all, the Kaduna refinery. Table 4.3 shows the products of the three refineries, some of which are consumed domestically and others exported to neighbouring African countries. Nigeria is a net importer of petroleum products. The products of the refineries are as follows:

Liquefied Petroleum Gas,
Aviation Spirit,
Motor Spirit,
Dual Purpose Kerosine,
Automotive Gas Oil,
Fuel Oil,
Lubricating Oil,
Greases,
Petroleum Jelly,
Waxes,
Bitumen and Asphalt.

Table 4.2: Nigeria's Crude Oil Production and Exports Statistics, 1958–80

Year	Production (barrels)	Exports (barrels)
1958	1,876,062	1,820,305
1959	4,095,611	3,957,446
1960	6,367,187	6,243,527
1961	16,801,896	16,505,985
1962	24,623,691	24,679,769
1963	27,913,479	27,701,320
1964	43,996,895	43,431,563
1965	99,353,794	96,984,975
1966	152,428,168	139,549,969
1967	116,553,292	109,274,902
1968	51,907,304	52,129,855
1969	197,204,486	197,245,641
1970	395,835,689	383,455,353
1971	558,678,882	542,545,131
1972	643,206,685	650,979,689
1973	750,593,415	723,313,837
1974	823,317,838	795,710,044
1975	651,506,761	627,638,983
1976	758,058,380	736,822,998
1977	766,053,944	744,413,355
1978	692,269,121	667,387,067
1979	842,474,109	813,726,843
1980	754,620,497	n.a.
1981	381,394,806[a]	n.a.
1982	474,500,000[a]	n.a.

Note: a. Estimates.

Source: Petroleum Inspectorate Annual Report (various issues) and CBN, *Annual Report and Statement of Accounts*, December, 1980.

Table 4.3: Nigeria's Refinery Production Returns — September, 1981

Products	Port Harcourt refinery Actual Production		Warri refinery Actual Production		Kaduna refinery Actual Production	
	Metric Tons	'000 Litres	Metric Tons	'000 Litres	Metric Tons	'000 Litres
Liquefied Petroleum Gases	—	—	—	—	618	1,093
Premium Motor Spirit	50,084	67,163	115,119	154,374	62,110	83,290
5 Star Motor Spirit	—	—	—	—	—	—
Dual Purpose Kerosine	34,138	46,564	52,929	65,209	20,181	26,095
Automotive Gas Oil	46,230	56,955	112,964	131,490	44,024	51,244
Low Pour Fuel Oil	12,930	15,050	46,881	49,225	17,330	18,197
High Pour Fuel Oil	71,570	76,795	—	—	—	—

Source: Nigerian National Petroleum Corporation, *Monthly Petroleum Information,* September, 1981.

Nigeria's consumption of petroleum products is expected to rise in the coming years. The Kaduna refinery has not yet attained full production capacity. From an estimated 3.68 million metric tonnes for domestic consumption in 1982, petrol consumption is expected to rise to 4.6 million metric tonnes by 1983. The increase in the prices of domestically consumed petroleum products announced in April, 1982 notwithstanding, petrol consumption is expected to rise to 1.95 million metric tonnes in 1983, 2.42 million metric tonnes in 1985 and 3.6 million metric tonnes in 1990. It is expected that there will be a reduction in the rate of kerosine consumption because of the rural electrification scheme, which many State governments are embarking upon. Liquefied petroleum gas is expected to rise tremendously by over 100 per cent after 1982. The projected consumption of liquefied petroleum gas (LPG) is estimated at 101,565 metric tonnes by 1990. Fuel oil used for power generation by NEPA and by the Kaduna refinery in particular is also expected to rise by over 100 per cent, even though the demand for fuel oil is far below the production capacities of the oil refinery. In 1981 only 243,124 metric tonnes of high power fuel oil were consumed. The refineries are finding it difficult to sell the surplus fuel oil.

4. Port Harcourt Refinery

The construction of Nigeria's first refinery at Alese-Eleme, located about ten kilometres from Port Harcourt in the Eastern part of the country was completed in October, 1965 and began operation in the same month. The objective of setting up the refinery was to reduce Nigeria's importation of petroleum products The refinery has a processing capacity of 38,000 barrels a day. When it started production, however, only 32,000 barrels a day of crude oil could be processed. A year after it had been commissioned the refinery attained its optimum capacity of 38,000 barrels a day. That notwithstanding, Nigeria still continued to import over 10 per cent of processed petroleum to augment the local production of the refinery and exported in turn about 100,000 barrels of petroleum derivatives, consisting mainly of surplus fuel oil which could not be consumed in Nigeria, and whose world market demand and price were very low. The fuel oil was therefore sold at low prices to willing buyers. The Alese refinery was equipped to produce a limited range of petroleum products such as motor gasoline (petroleum) and aviation turbine fuel, gas diesel oil and fuel oil. The refinery does not produce such petroleum products as lubricants, bitumen, aviation gasoline and other petroleum products. The production of aviation gasoline requires high quality control and the demand is very low in Nigeria. Moreover, airlines were switching over from the use of aviation gasoline to the use of aviation turbine. The low level of industrialisation also limited the demand for lubricants, which were not produced at the Alese-Eleme refinery. The production of bitumen was ruled out because of the low sulphur content of Nigeria's brand of crude oil.

These products which were not in much demand in Nigeria were therefore imported from other refineries which processed crude oil with a high sulphur content. During the Nigeria/Biafra war which began in 1967 and ended in January, 1970, Nigeria's sole refinery was badly damaged and was only resuscitated in the latter part of 1970; by that time Nigeria's demand for petroleum products such as gasoline, aviation turbine, fuel and motor spirit had exceeded the capacity of the existing refinery. It became necessary to plan for more refineries, which were to be located at Warri in the Western part of the country and at Kaduna in the Northern part of the country. The new refineries were to be designed to produce petroleum products currently demanded in the Nigerian market and to minimise the production of petroleum derivatives, such as fuel oil, for which the Alese-Eleme refinery had surplus capacity. The demand for fuel oil in Nigeria was in decline as the National Electric Power Authority (NEPA) was quickly replacing power generation through fuel oil with the hydro system. The multimillion naira Kainji dam built to generate hydroelectricity was expected to replace the thermal power stations of NEPA at Ijora-Lagos and other regional stations. The Ijora NEPA thermal station and others located in parts of the country which normally used fuel oil for the generation of electricity were no longer put to full use. This led to a loss of domestic demand for Nigerian fuel oil.

The two new refineries planned for Warri and Kaduna were therefore expected to produce enough to meet Nigeria's traditional demands for petroleum products and to satisfy new demands occasioned by Nigeria's rapid infrastructural and industrial development. The Warri refinery was designed to process Nigeria's crude oil with a low sulphur content while the Kaduna refinery was expected to process imported heavy crudes with a high sulphur content from which would be obtained petroleum derivatives such as lubricating oils, asphalt, waxes, liquid petroleum gas, gasoline (petrol), kerosine, gas oil (diesel oil), fuel oil and sulphur. The heavy crudes had to be imported from Kuwait, Saudi Arabia or Venezuela. Finally, Nigeria decided to import the heavy crude oil required for the Kaduna refinery complex from Venezuela.

5. Kaduna Refinery

Of the three refineries Port Harcourt, Warri and Kaduna, the Kaduna refinery which was commissioned and completed in 1980 is the largest and the most complex. It is also considered as one of the largest refineries in Africa and it provides Nigeria with a firm foundation for the establishment of petrochemical industries. The project was conceived in 1974, a time when there was an acute fuel shortage in Nigeria because of the limited production capacity of the Port Harcourt refinery. The Kaduna refinery was initially designed for a capacity of 60,000 bpsd (barrels per stream day) but to begin with it had an actual processing production capacity of 42,000 bpsd. Later the plant was redesigned with a total capacity of 100,000 bpsd, at an estimated cost of N468 million.

The project was designed by NNPC engineers in conjunction with a consulting firm, King Wilkinson of the Netherlands, following a series of feasibility studies conducted by them. The contract to build the refinery was awarded in 1977 to Chiyoda Chemical Engineering and Construction Company Limited of Yokohama, Japan and was based on an international tender exercise. The Kaduna refinery processes both Nigeria's light crude and the imported heavy crude with high sulphur content. The Nigerian crude yields fuel products while the imported heavy crude yields in addition to fuel products, lubricating oils, waxes and asphalt.

The refinery has two sections, the Lubes Processing Unit and the Fuel Processing Unit. Both have a processing capacity of 100,000 barrels of crude oil per day. The refinery has a tank farm consisting of 165 giant tanks for storing both processed petroleum products and raw materials. The refinery can produce over four million tonnes of fuel and related derivatives. The Lubes Unit processes about 50,000 barrels of Nigerian light crude oil and produces mainly fuel (white products) such as liquefied petroleum gas (LPG), five star gasoline (FSG), super grade gasoline (SGG), dual purpose kerosine (DPK), gas oil (GO) and fuel oil (FO). Liquefied petroleum gas (LPG) is a gas which is liquefied, stored in cylinders and used for cooking. By releasing the pressure, the liquid is converted into gas. LPG is also used for metal cutting and as a refrigerant in refrigerators. The fuel oil produced by the refinery is used for generating electricity for the refinery which has an independent power supply plant of 42 mega-watts strength. In the case of the Kaduna refinery the fuel oil is put to economic use. The waxes produced by the Lube Unit from the heavy imported crude oil are used for the making of candles, match sticks, waterproof papers, cardboard packaging, insulators for the electrical and electronic industries, carbon paper and typewriter ribbons. Asphalt, one of the derivatives of the Kaduna refinery, is of much importance for the construction of a road network envisaged for the country. The sulphur from the plant will be used by the Super

Figure 4.1: NNPC Refineries, Products Pipeline Network, Depots and Pumpstations

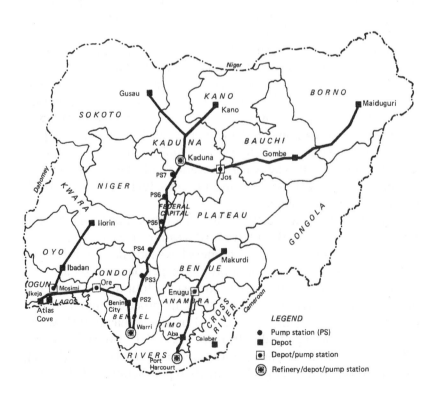

Phosphate Company in Kaduna for the manufacture of fertiliser.

In addition to the main products of the refinery, subsidiary companies have been set up to support the refinery. The Drum Manufacturing Company will produce about 8,000 drums per day and is the second largest Drum Company in the world. The Tin Manufacturing Company will produce about 22,400 tins per hour for the storage of kerosine in particular. The Wax Moulding Packaging Company will cut the waxes into sizes and package them for market.

The companies' products are evacuated through pipelines, road and rail. Products to be evacuated mainly through pipelines are gasoline, kerosine and gas oil. About 75 per cent of these products are evacuated through pipelines as shown in Figure 4.1, while 25 per cent of each of them is evacuated in bulk by road. About 60 per cent of LPG is evacuated bulk by road and 40 per cent bulk by rail; fuel oil 50 per cent bulk by road and 50 per cent bulk by rail, and lubricating oil 40 per cent bulk by road and 60 per cent bulk by rail. Asphalt is evacuated 50 per cent bulk by rail and 25 per cent by road and rail respectively. Sulphur is evacuated 50 per cent bulk by road and 50 per cent bulk by rail while wax is evacuated 50 per cent by road and rail through the use of drums or packages.

6. Nigeria's Natural Gas

Natural gas is available in Nigeria in large quantities. There are two types of gas reserves in Nigeria, associated and non-associated gas. Associated gas is found in the course of crude oil production. It is produced with the oil. Non-associated gas on the other hand exists freely in traps and is not connected with crude oil production. As crude oil production in Nigeria increases so also does the level of associated gas which accompanies it. As of 1981, the estimated natural gas reserves in Nigeria were about 88 trillion standard cubic feet of gas or the equivalent of 15 billion barrels of crude oil. Out of these reserves, associated gas constitutes approximately 20 per cent while non-associated gas constitutes 80 per cent of Nigeria's natural gas reserves. In Nigerian oil fields about 90 per cent of the associated gas is flared and only some 10 per cent is put into commercial use. Until recently there was no clear-cut government policy on the exploration of Nigeria's natural gas. This does not mean that Nigerian policy makers are ignorant of the importance of gas as an alternative energy source. The absence until 1979 of governmental policy on the utilisation of Nigeria's natural gas was partly due to a number of economic and technical problems.

(i) Economic and Technical Arguments Against Gas

Exploitation in Nigeria

The main economic argument was that industrial and household

Table 4.4: Ongoing Gas Contracts and Projected Industrial Gas Requirement

Ongoing Gas Contracts

Consumers	Contract Quantity
Nigerian Breweries Ltd.	0.240 MMCFD
Associated Industries Ltd. Aba	0.850 MMCFD
Lever Brothers Aba	0.528 MMCFD
International Equitables, Aba	0.144 MMCFD
Aba Textile Mills	1.500 MMCFD
International Glass Industries, Aba	1.200 MMCFD
RSUB, Port Harcourt	1.800 MMCFD
NPRC, Alesa-Eleme	7.200 MMCFD
Bendel Glass, Ughelli	0.850 MMCFD
Delta Glass, Ughelli	2.240 MMCFD
NEPA, Ughelli	90.000 MMCFD
NEPA, Afam	90.000 MMCFD
NEPA, Sapele	120.000 MMCFD
Total	316.552

Projects Being Proposed or
Being Actively Prosecuted

Project	Average Daily Gas Requirement
Liquefied Natural Gas (LNG)	2,000 MMCFD
Aladja Steel Plant	70 MMCFD
Ajaokuta Steel Complex	200 MMCFD
NEPA, Lagos Power Station (with provision for Industrial Consumers)	400 MMCFD
NEPA, Afam IV Extension	140 MMCFD
NEPA, Sapele Phase II	150 MMCFD
Abuja (Federal Capital Territory Projected Need)	100 MMCFD
Onne Nitrogenous Fertilizer Plant	65 MMCFD
Warri Refinery	30 MMCFD
Total	3,155

Source: *NAPETCOR*, October–December, 1981, pp. 6-7.

demand for gas in Nigeria was not significant enough to warrant investments of billions of naira in the gas industry. The low demand for natural gas was attributed mainly to the climatic conditions of Nigeria. Nigeria lies in the tropics; it enjoys an abundance of sunlight, and therefore requires no gas for heating purposes quite unlike countries that lie in the temperate zone. The Nigerian population concentrates more in the rural areas where firewood for cooking purposes abounds. The majority of Nigerians are therefore unlikely to discard a cheap (and free) traditional source of energy for an expensive modern one.

Nigerian industries on the other hand prefer the use of petroleum as a source of energy: it is available at all times and, very importantly, petroleum is subsidised by the government and is therefore cheap. Clearly there was no immediate pressure to change to another energy system. The oil companies themselves considered the exploitation of gas less profitable that the more lucrative crude oil which offers a greater profit base. Table 4.4 shows the ongoing contracts and projected industrial gas requirement in Nigeria for the period 1978-9, while 4.5a shows gas utilised and flared by producing companies in the month of September, 1981 alone.

A number of arguments of a technical nature have been advanced to show that the cost of extracting the gas and distributing it would be enormous. First of all, the gas fields are small and dispersed over large areas in the Niger Delta regions of Nigeria. This makes it difficult for

Table 4.5a: Gas Utilised and Gas Flared by Producing Companies — September, 1981

Name of oil field	Gas used as fuel (in cubic metres)	Gas flared (in cubic metres)
Shell	6,193,636	551,549,238
Gulf	2,601,000	179,661
Mobil	3,147,000	43,220,000
Agip	905,840	—
Phillips	37,068	3,420,223
Ashland	35,040	11,130,960
Texaco	337,000	13,177,000
Pan Ocean	454,488	991,884
Elf	33,063,540	32,469,950
Total	46,774,612	836,553,108

Source: Nigerian National Petroleum Corporation, *Monthly Petroleum Information*, September, 1981.

the gas to be collected cheaply and in commercial quantities. Because of the scattered nature of the gas fields and the high cost of collecting them the oil companies have no alternative but to flare them as the cost of oil production is far cheaper than laying adequate gas pipelines to connect the gas fields. It thus became reasonable to invest the large amount of capital which should have been used for the gas industry into the oil production industry. City demand for gas was also considered too small to merit the laying of gas pipes to the cities. Industrial and household consumption of gas in Nigeria was considered insufficient to justify such an enormous investment.

(ii) Arguments In Favour of Gas Exploitation

A considerable number of Nigerian experts consider it wasteful to flare the gas when it should be harnessed for the benefit of the economy. They argue that if the industrial and household demand in Nigeria is not adequate then Nigerian gas should be liquefied and exported to the markets of Europe and the United States where demand is much higher. It was felt that the government should generate a policy to increase the use of gas for power generation in Nigeria, especially as the hydro systems used for power generation in Nigeria have constantly developed technical problems which frequently led to power rationing for both industry and households. It has also been argued that Nigeria should not rely solely on crude oil as the main foreign exchange earner, because if world market prices for crude oil drop drastically, as was the case in 1982, and if OPEC reduces Nigeria's production quota, then it would be impossible for Nigeria to carry out its planned development programmes and maintain adequate imports to sustain normal consumer and industrial demands. The export of natural gas, therefore, should provide Nigeria with an alternative source of foreign exchange earnings and a diversification of the Nigerian economy. Naturally, gas as a primary source of energy is considered more efficient than electricity and to environmentalists it minimises air pollution as gas pipelines through which the gas flows are buried underground. In terms of revenue, the amount of gas flared every year is estimated at ₦1.5 billion. This is too large an amount to be ignored. Another argument in favour of the exploitation of Nigerian gas fields, in spite of the initial high cost of investment, is that the multibillion naira iron and steel projects which are currently under construction will require the use of gas in various aspects of their operations. Apart from the use of gas to generate more power for Nigeria's industries and for domestic consumption, it can also be used in fertiliser and petrochemical projects.

There is a strong need to develop the gas industry. Gas provides Nigeria with a long-term energy option, and gas, along with coal and oil, will provide Nigeria with optimum energy resources. The different areas of the economy which can best be served through the use of oil, gas or coal will benefit respectively through such energy diversification. Other possible sources of energy for Nigeria include geothermal, biomass, hydro, wind, solar and nuclear energy. Of all these only the hydro energy sources have been relatively developed. The rest are still undeveloped or undergoing experimentation and it will take many years before they can be put into economic use. Until then Nigeria will continue to depend on the three energy sources (i.e. oil, gas and coal) to cater for a very fast growing economy. A fast growing economy such as Nigeria's should have a good mix of energy sources. Should the industrial and domestic demand for gas be inadequate to warrant the construction of a national gas grid, the present industrial and domestic demand for gas through the use of liquefied petroleum gas (LPG) in cylinders should be encouraged until the industrial and domestic demand for gas has risen to a level consistent with the laying of gas pipelines from Nigerian gas fields to the cities. Until then the flaring of gas should be discontinued. It should rather be stored underground and conserved for future use.

7. Associated Gas Reinjection Decree (1979)

Arguments in favour of gas exploitation in Nigeria were too strong for the Federal Government of Nigeria to ignore. It became imperative for the Federal Government to formulate a gas policy in the interests of the Nigerian economy. Consequently the *Associated Gas Reinjection Decree* of 1979 was introduced. By this decree every oil and gas production company operating in Nigeria was requested to present a proposal to show the viable utilisation of associated gas from Nigeria's oil fields and to suggest projects in which associated gas not then utilised could be reinjected. The proposals where expected to be submitted before the 1 October 1980. The decree made it an offence for any oil or gas company to flare associated gas or non-associated gas after 1 January 1984, unless such a company had written permission from the Commissioner (Minister) in charge of Petroleum. Any gas company which acted contrary to the decree was likely to forfeit its licence or lease. Decree No. 99 was the first decisive step taken by the Federal Government towards the formulation of a coherent gas policy.

8. Proposals for the Future Utilisation of Gas in Nigeria

Studies reveal that the Nigerian economy will benefit immediately on two fronts — the domestic and external fronts. Through the use of gas for domestic power generation, a reasonable amount of Nigerian gas is expected to be consumed.

About 95 per cent of all gas sold in Nigeria is consumed by NEPA thermal stations and the trend is expected to continue. The Liquefied National Gas (LNG) project, which is a major project of the Fourth National Development Plan (1981 to 1985) for liquefying gas and transporting it in refrigerated ocean tankers for export to Europe and the US, will earn for Nigeria as much foreign exchange as crude oil. On reaching Europe or the US the liquefied gas is regasified and distributed through the importing country's gas pipeline grid to its domestic and industrial markets.

Table 4.5b shows the consumption of fuel and energy in the Nigerian economy from 1972 to 1980. The increasing importance of gas as a source of fuel and energy is becoming obvious. Since 1978, gas has overtaken hydropower as Nigeria's second largest source of fuel and energy. The importance will even be greater in 1989 when the LNG project is expected to be completed. Nigerian gas experts argue that the projected consumption of NEPA's thermal station, which is expected to be completed in Lagos by 1984, will consume about 300 MMSCFD (million standard cubic feet per day of gas).

Similar thermal power stations are also being planned. These stations will be linked by pipelines from the gas fields to constitute the first phase of Nigeria's gas pipeline grid. The pipelines supplying the thermal stations will also satisfy the demand of consumers inhabiting the areas of the pipeline route.

9. Proposed Gas Transmission Lines

The Nigeria National Petroleum Company surveyed the first phase of Nigeria's Gas Pipelines systems. One of the systems will transport gas from the gas fields of the Eastern States and deliver them to the proposed Liquefied National Gas Plant (LNG) at Bonny. Another sys-

Table 4.5b: Consumption of Fuel and Energy

Sources	1972 Consumption (Tonnes)	% Share	1973 Consumption (Tonnes)	% Share	1974 Consumption (Tonnes)	% Share	1975 Consumption (Tonnes)	% Share	1976 Consumption (Tonnes)	% Share
Petroleum products	2,970,627	67.0	3,573,066	71.0	4,115,786	69.0	4,910,606	70.0	7,324,861	73.9
Hydropower	809,279	19.0	898,456	18.0	1,064,670	18.0	1,342,859	19.0	1,250,956	12.6
Natural gas	365,826	8.0	328,548	6.0	541,686	9.0	618,216	9.0	1,119,135	11.3
Coal	271,489	6.0	274,463	5.0	240,643	4.0	182,705	2.0	218,226	2.2
Total	4,417,221	100.0	5,074,533	100.0	5,962,785	100.0	7,054,386	100.0	9,913,178	100.0
Index of Energy Consumption (1972 = 100)	100		115		135		160		205	

Sources	1977 Consumption (Tonnes)	% Share	1978 Consumption (Tonnes)	% Share	1979 Consumption (Tonnes)	% Share	1980a Consumption (Tonnes)	% Share
Petroleum products	8,529,107	74.5	9,805,536	78.5	10,195,704	74.0	11,946,320	77.3
Hydropower	1,538,985	13.5	1,003,375	8.0	1,580,802	11.5	1,461,817	9.5
Natural gas	1,160,705	10.1	1,483,026	11.9	1,848,754	13.4	1,918,901	12.4
Coal	221,896	1.9	192,970	1.6	148,703	0.8	128,107	0.8
Total	11,450,693	100.0	2,484,907	100.0	13,773,963	100.0	15,455,145	100.0
Index of Energy Consumption (1972 = 100)	283.1		321.9		337.2		393.2	

Note: a. Provisional.

Source: CBN, *Annual Report and Statement of Accounts*, December, 1978 and December, 1980.

tem will connect gas fields at Uzere, Olomoro, Oweh, Eriemu, Kokori, Afiesere, Ugheli and Utorogu for use at the Alaga Delta Steel Complex which is expected to consume about 70 MMSCFD of gas. The last is nearing completion and gas flaring in the area is expected to terminate by the end of 1982. The second system, also in the Bendel State of Nigeria, will carry gas from the Escravos gas field to the NEPA thermal power station at Sapelle which is expected to consume 150 MMSCFD of gas in the first phase although the installed capacity has a consumption capacity of 270 MMSCFD. As power demand in Nigeria increases the gas consumption of the thermal stations is bound to increase. The same grid which supplies the NEPA station at Sapele will also deliver gas to the Iron and Steel Complex at Ajaokuta, the NEPA thermal station at Lagos under construction and the new Federal Capital at Abuja in the Northern part of the country. These gas pipeline systems are expected to be completed before the end of the Fourth National Development Plan in 1985. When the transmission systems are completed there will be no reason to continue to flare gas. When the transmission lines become fully operational Nigeria will have taken a giant step towards proper utilisation of one of Nigeria's most important energy sources which until the latter part of the 1970s had been completely ignored.

The gas transmission systems which are under construction are estimated to cost about ₦2 billion. The project will be funded mainly by NNPC which has a monopoly of the gas transmission systems. NNPC is likely to invite other oil and gas companies to participate in the project or to enter into joint venture agreements with them. The Petroleum Inspectorate Division of NNPC will be in charge of the gas transmisson lines which will transport an estimated 2.1 billion cubic feet of gas per day to the various terminals mentioned above.

10. The Nigerian Liquefied Natural Gas Project (LNG)

A number of proposals have been made concerning the commercialisation of Nigeria's gas. One of them is the recovery of natural gas liquids from gas stream. This will enable the liquefication of petroleum gas and the extraction of ethane for the petrochemical industries. The process will yield reasonable revenue but it is considered inappropriate because it will only allow for the utilisation of 10 per cent of the gas stream.

Another proposal which would allow the chemical upgrading of natural gas for the production of ammonia and methanol for the Fertiliser Industry received little enthusiasm because of the low consumption of gas. However, the project has not been completely dropped. It is still under consideration in view of the fact that Nigeria spends millions of naira every year to import fertiliser from other countries. If fertiliser projects are established, Nigeria will save millions of naira in foreign exchange which is currently being spent every year on the importation of fertiliser. In the long run Nigeria may turn out to be a net exporter of fertiliser.

The proposal which has been approved under the Fourth National Development Plan is that of exporting liquefied gas to Europe, the United States and Japan where the industrial and domestic demand for gas is very high. Liquefied gas is a major foreign exchange earner in countries like Algeria, Indonesia and Abu Dhabi. These countries are also oil exporting countries like Nigeria. Algeria supplies liquefied gas to the United Kingdom, France, Spain and the United States. Libya supplies to Italy and Spain and Indonesia supplies mainly to Japan. Abu Dhabi also supplies mainly to Japan. The total production of liquefied natural gas (LNG) of Algeria is about 1,700 million daily gas volume. Libya produces about 350 million daily gas volume of liquefied natural gas. Indonesia on the other hand produces about 1,850 million daily gas volume while Abu Dhabi produces 450 million gas volume.

The LNG project under construction in Nigeria, which is expected to be completed in 1989, is of the base-load type. This involves the liquefication of gas and the use of refrigerated ocean tankers to carry liquefied gas to foreign markets where it is regasified and distributed through the gas pipeline grid of the importing country. Nigeria's LNG project is expected to go into operation before 1985 and to produce for export about 12.7 billion cubic feet of gas daily.

In order to ensure that the project was realised a joint venture company called the Bonny LNG was formed by the Nigerian Federal Government in 1978. Co-operating in the project are a total of five oil companies registered in Nigeria, the other four being Shell (now called African Petroleum), Phillips, Agip, and Elf. The Bonny LNG company is authorised to purchase gas from the Nigerian National Petroleum Company for liquefication and sale to Western Europe and America. Bechtel National Incorporated of San-Francisco, USA, which has an international reputation in the construction of LNG projects is involved in the Nigerian scheme.

The Federal Government has also engaged the services of three

North American firms as consultants. These firms will carry out an independent study on the viability of the project. The World Bank has already carried out a feasibility study of the project. Arthur D. Little, a famous project economist, has been commissioned to review the economic aspects of the project. While the New York based First Boston Corporation undertakes the financial evaluation of the project, legal matters will be dealt with by Sherman and Stirling. Local Consultants have also been engaged to ensure that local conditions are taken into account by the same foreign consultants. The Federal Government has engaged the services of the International Merchant Bankers (Nig.) Ltd. to look into the financial aspects of the project and Skoup Associated Consultants, headed by a well-known Nigerian economist Pius Okigbo, are to evaluate the economic issues of the project in conjunction with Arthur D. Little. The consultants are expected to submit their report before the end of 1982, so that the three-train gas liquefying plant can take off immediately. The present world oil glut emphasises the importance of the LNG project as an alternative foreign exchange earner. The first stage of the project is expected to produce 8,000 million cubic metres of gas a year while the second phase of the project which is expected to be completed by 1989 will begin producing at full capacity as from 1990.

11. Other Sources of Primary Power and Energy

Apart from hydrocarbon (crude oil and natural gas), Nigeria is blessed with solid fuels such as coal, bitumite and hydropower sources.

(i) Coal

Large surveys indicate the existence of large deposits of sub-bituminous coal in Southern Nigeria especially in the Enugu and Benue river areas. Coal is one of the oldest Nigerian minerals and the main reserves are in the magnitude of 360 million tonnes. Nigerian coal is not of high quality although it is said to have a caloric strength of about 6,000 calories per gramme and to contain a reasonable quantity of sulphur, but it cannot be coked. The market for coal has declined both in Nigeria and abroad. The main consumers of Nigerian coal are the Nigerian Railway Corporation, Niger Cement Corporation, Nkalagu, and Ghana. These market sources have declined considerably in the last decade. The Nigerian Railway Corporation has a long-term plan to switch over from locomotive to diesel engines. The Niger Cement Corporation was crippled by a power struggle and was out of production for almost nine months during 1981–2. Other domestic consumers are also switching over to other energy sources. Coal is a potential solid fuel for Nigeria but, because of other alternatives now available, coal as a source of energy is still to be fully exploited.

(ii) Bitumite

The main reserves of bitumite are calculated at between 150 million tonnes to 300 million tonnes. It is found in the Asaba area in Bendel State, Gongola Division in Bauchi State, Nnewi in Anambra State and Aba and Owerri in Imo State of Nigeria. Bitumite is not currently used in Nigeria as a source of fuel but its potential is said to be enormous.

(iii) Hydropower

Nigeria is rich in hydro-sources of electric power. Hydro-sources of electric power are found on the River Niger and the tributaries of Benue and Kaduna. The oldest hydroelectric power stations in Nigeria are operated by NESCO (Nigeria Electricity Supply Company) and the main consumers of the power generated by NESCO are the mines around Jos in the Plateau State of Nigeria. The first hydropower station was built in 1923 at Kwali Falls by NESCO. The largest hydropower station in Nigeria is the Kainji Dam on the River Niger which began operation with four hydroelectric generators and a total capacity of 320 megawatts. Kainji Dam has provision for 12 hydroelectric generators. More hydropower sources are planned for Nigeria.

(iv) Other Possible Sources of Energy

Other potential sources of energy in Nigeria are uranium, solar and wind energy. These sources are still to be exploited and harnessed for use in Nigeria. Uranium is a radioactive material found in small quantities in several parts of Northern Nigeria, especially in the Kastina area and North Eastern part of Kano State. Already, the Nigerian Federal Government has set up a uranium mining company to exploit uranium deposits in partnership with foreign companies. Solar energy is currently being investigated. The University of Nigeria has received a grant of about ₦4 million to investigate and research into the use of solar energy in Nigeria, especially its applications in the rural areas where electrification had not been extended. The successful development and application of solar energy will be of immense benefit to the country and will constitute an inexhaustible source of energy for the country. Wind energy is also being investigated, particularly with regard to its use for irrigation purposes.

Table 4.6 shows the sources of primary energy and power in Nigeria according to their known reserves, probable reserves and possible reserves. The Federal Government is currently formulating a policy on future energy options for Nigeria. There is no doubt that these sources are going to be taken into serious consideration in deciding which energy option or a mix of options will satisfy Nigeria's future household and industrial demands for energy and power.

There is also no doubt that gas will be Nigeria's second largest source of household and industrial energy. Since 1978 natural gas consumption has ranked next to petroleum products in Nigeria's energy mix. Table 4.5b is a convincing testimony to the future role of natural gas in the Nigerian economy.

Table 4.6: Sources of Primary Energy and Power in Nigeria

	Known reserves	Probable reserves	Possible reserves
1. Hydrocarbons			
Crude oil (10^6 tons)	200	600	1,200
Natural gas (10^9 m^3)	280	400	800
Shales & Sands (bituminous)	not estimated	not estimated	not estimated
2. Solid Fuels			
Coal (10^6 tons)	360	500	800
Lignite (10^6 tons)	75	150	300
3. Nuclear Fuels			
$U_3 O_8$ (10^3 tons)	indications	indications	indications
$Th O_2$ (10^3 tons)	15	20	25
4. Hydroelectric Potential			
(10^9 kWh per annum)	17	20	20

Source: *Energy Resources and Utilisation*, MOURTADA DIALLO;
Conference on National Reconstruction and Development in Nigeria, 1969.

References and Additional Reading

Akpe, S.M., 'Utilising Nigeria's Natural Gas', in *NAPETCOR*, vol. 2, no. 4, Oct.-Dec., 1981

'Conservation of Nigeria's Petroleum Resources', in the *Nigerian Statesman*, Owerri, Nigeria, 21 Sep. 1980

'Crude Oil Production and Export Figures for April Out', in the *NNPC News*, June, 1981

Diallo, M., *Energy Resources and Utilization*, Speech at the Conference on National Reconstruction and Development, Ibadan, March, 1969

Ekpo, O., 'Natural Gas — Options for Nigeria', in *NAPETCOR*, vol. 2, no. 1, Jan.–March, 1981

'Fuel From Crude Oil', in the *Daily Times*, Lagos, Nigeria, 5 March 1980

'Government Now Determined on LNG', in the *Business Times*, Lagos, Nigeria, 3 May 1982

'Kaduna Refinery: A Step in the Right Direction', in the *Daily Times*, Lagos, Nigeria, 5 March 1980

'Kaduna Refinery Lube Plant Starts Production Soon', in the *NNPC News*, Lagos, Nigeria, May, 1981

Mercier, C., *The Petrochemical Industry and the Possibilities of its Establishment in the Developing Countries*, Editions Techniq, Paris, 1966

NNPC, 'Kaduna Refinery', in *NAPETCOR*, vol. 1, no. 1, Oct.-Dec., 1980

NNPC, *NNPC Refinery in Kaduna*, Public Affairs Department, NNPC, Lagos

'NNPC Laboratory in PH', in the *NNPC News*, Lagos, Nigeria, May, 1981

'Nigeria and the Energy Situation', in the *Business Times*, Lagos, Nigeria, 7 Oct. 1980

'Oil Production Drops Further', in the *Business Times*, Lagos, Nigeria, 29 March 1982

Schatzl, L., *Selected Aspects of the Nigerian Energy Economy*, Nigerian Institute of Social and Economic Research, Ibadan, March, 1969

'The Nigerian LNG Project', in the *Daily Times*, Lagos, Nigeria, 8 Sep. 1981

5 THE IMPACT OF OIL ON THE NIGERIAN ECONOMY

There is no doubt that the oil industry has contributed tremendously to the overall growth of Nigeria's economy. Nigeria is considered the fastest developing country in black Africa. This description of Nigeria would have been impossible if the impact of the oil industry on the Nigerian economy over the last two decades is discounted. The prospects of further positive effects on the economy are very bright in view of the enormous oil reserves in Nigeria. Currently the oil industry contributes over 90 per cent of Nigeria's national income and over 85 per cent of Federal Government revenue. Nigeria's Gross Domestic Fixed Capital Formation (GDFCF) has also experienced a tremendous growth during the last decade because of the oil industry. From a country persistently in deficit in its balance of payments during the 1950s and 1960s, Nigeria is now a country with surplus reserves — because of the oil industry. In manpower training and technological transfer as well, the oil industry has accounted for positive and beneficial changes in the economy.

One may not readily appreciate the impact of oil exports on Nigeria's balance of payments and reserve positions until the contributions of oil and non-oil exports to Nigeria's balance of payments positions are analysed. Nigeria's external reserves have also grown over the years although there was a substantial fall in the 1981/2 period because of the low production quota assigned to Nigeria by OPEC following the world oil glut.

1. Income Effects

Until 1958 when the first oil exports were made totalling 1.8 million barrels (about the current daily production) oil had no impact on the Nigerian economy. By 1980 only about 51.3 million barrels of crude oil were processed and consumed annually in Nigeria. Nigeria consumes less than 10 per cent of its total annual oil production. The remainder is sold at world market prices and the receipts add to Nigeria's national income. From Table 5.1 it can be seen clearly that the GDP of Nigeria rose phenomenally between 1970 and 1980. This

Table 5.1: Oil and Non-oil Capital Flows into Nigeria
(₦ million)

Year	Oil	Non-Oil	Total
1960	+ 24.8	+ 29.4	+ 54.2
1961	+ 13.6	+ 50.4	+ 64.0
1962	+ 6.6	+ 23.2	+ 29.8
1963	+ 10.4	+ 58.8	+ 69.2
1964	+ 36.2	+ 111.4	+ 147.6
1965	+ 34.8	+ 97.2	+ 132.0
1966	+ 57.8	+ 39.0	+ 96.8
1967	+ 91.0	+ 31.8	+ 122.8
1968	+ 59.8	+ 100.2	+ 160.0
1969	− 33.4	+ 140.0	+ 80.6
1970	− 130.4	+ 179.6	+ 49.2
1971	+ 4.0	+ 289.4	+ 293.4
1972	+ 195.8	+ 63.4	+ 259.2
1973	+ 64.5	− 5.3	+ 59.2
1974	+ 135.8	− 141.7	− 5.9
1975	+ 121.4	+ 19.7	+ 141.1
1976	− 42.0	− 8.6	− 50.6
1977	+ 147.5	+ 86.9	+ 234.4

Source: CBN, Extracted from 'Summary of Balance of Payments of
Nigeria', in *Economic and Financial Review,* December, 1978, pp. 6-7.

coincides with the period in which there was greater activity in crude
oil production and also in the export of crude oil. Currently crude oil
contributes to over 90 per cent of Nigeria's national income because
of a decline in Nigeria's traditional export products such as cocoa,
palm produce, groundnuts and timber. This is considered unfortun-
ate. Should Nigeria's oil reserves be depleted it is feared that the
economy would collapse in the absence of diversification. The agricultural sector which had been the main engine of the economy has
been relegated to the background. This sector now contributes less
than 10 per cent of Nigeria's national income. Until the economy is
diversified and agriculture and manufacturing emphasised, Nigeria
will continue as a monocultural economy dependent on the oil industry.

2. Capital Formation

Table 5.1, extracted from Nigeria's Balance of Payments Statistics

Table 5.2: Public Oil Sector Projects in the Third National Development Plan, 1975-80

Title of Project	(₦ millions)	
	Original Plan Estimate	Latest Revised Estimate as at 1977/8
NOMCO		
National Oil Marketing Company Ltd. (NOMCO)	25	10.00 (Unipetrol Acquisition & Equity)
NOMCO Distribution and Storage Facilities		
(a) Depots	42	206.00
(b) Products Pipeline	300	345.00
The National Oil Marketing Company Tanker Subsidiary	234	160.00 Merged with (a) and (b) above
NNPC		
NNPC Direct Exploration activities	270	27.00
Joint Venture Activities		
(a) Consideration for acquisition of interest in oil producing companies	542	542.00
(b) Capital Funding	617	617.00
(c) Exploration Companies	116	—
(d) Production sharing contracts —		
(i) Ashland	45	—
(ii) Other production sharing contracts	60	—
Joint Service Companies	10	10.00
NNPC Headquarters	30	3.00
Petroleum Training Institute and Crude Analysis Laboratory		
(a) Petroleum Train. Inst.	10	
(b) Other buildings	8	44.0
(c) Equipment & Expansion	7	
NNPC contribution to host communities	5.3	5.30
Building projects of the Dept. of Petroleum Resources	0.50	Merged with NNPC HQ
Manpower Development	5	Merged with PTI
Warri Refinery	160	478.00
Port Harcourt Refinery (Extension)	5	10.00
Kaduna Refinery	190	504.00
Export Refineries	376	—
A lube oil & Asphalt Plant	12	Merged with Kaduna Refinery
LNG Plants	1,260	1,260.00
Gas Supply — Sapele Gas	—	26.80
Total	4,534.8	4,491.1

Source: NNPC, *Progress of Public Sector Participation in the Nigerian Oil Industry*, September 1978, p. 7.

covering the period 1960-77, shows the oil and non-oil capital inflow from outside to the Nigerian economy. From the Table, it can be seen that oil capital experienced some decline between the period 1969-70, that is during the Nigeria/Biafra war, and in 1976 when oil companies disinvested slightly in preparation for the first oil glut which was expected in 1977. Capital inflow to the non-oil sector declined in 1973, 1974 and 1976. Table 5.2 shows capital projects of the oil industry as programmed for the Third National Development Plan which ended in 1980. The oil industry is very capital intensive. If the oil industry continues to provide Nigeria with about 90 per cent of her national income, it stands to reason that most of the nation's fixed investment will continue to be concentrated in the oil sector.

It is not possible here to quantify capital formation of the oil industry arising from land and land development, building and construction and manpower developments. There is no doubt however that it is significant. In the area of manpower development alone, NNPC and other oil companies are training a number of Nigerians in the various specialised areas of the oil industry. The Petroleum Institute at Warri also provides a training centre for middle-level oil manpower required by the Nigerian oil industry.

3. Monetary Arena

It has been empirically established that the oil producing countries have very high annual growth rates of money supply. It has also been empirically established that Nigeria's growth of money supply is one of the fastest among the oil producing countries.

The rapid growth rate of the money supply in Nigeria can be attributed to the activities of both private and public sectors of the economy. Money creation in the private sector emanates mainly from bank credit to the private sector and to the net foreign exchange earnings of the private sector. The public sector on the other hand contributes to Nigeria's growth of money supply through domestic spending by the government and its agencies. The Government contributes to the growth of money supply through the expenditure of revenue generated from domestic sources such as direct and indirect taxes; sale of government debt instruments (i.e., treasury bills and certificates and bonds) and bank credit. Through the monetisation of foreign exchange by government, the money supply is also expanded. In the 1960s revenue from traditional domestic sources and bank credit constituted the main base for monetary creation in Nigeria by the public sector. At that time, bank credit and foreign exchange earnings in the private sector contributed most to money supply. Today the reverse is the case. While the public sector contribution to money supply has increased dramatically, the contribution of the private sector has tended to decline.

On further analysis the main contribution in the public sector to money supply in the 1970s has been the monetisation of a large portion of foreign exchange proceeds which accrued from the sale of oil for the purpose of carrying out some aspects of the development programmes of the government. The Federal and State governments are the biggest spenders in the Nigerian economy and most of the money which they spend comes from oil proceeds. One can conclude very firmly that oil money influences very strongly the overall level of supply in the economy. An empirical test is bound to establish a

Table 5.3: Nigeria's Export Statistics, 1960-80

Year	Oil (₦ million)	Non oil (₦ million)	% of Oil to Total Exports
1960	8.8	321.2	2.7
1961	23.1	323.8	6.7
1962	33.5	300.7	10.0
1963	40.4	331.1	10.9
1964	64.1	365.1	14.9
1965	136.2	400.6	25.4
1966	189.9	384.3	32.4
1967	144.8	338.8	29.9
1968	74.0	348.2	17.5
1969	261.9	374.4	41.2
1970	510.0	375.4	57.6
1971	953.0	340.3	73.7
1972	1,176.2	258.0	82.0
1973	1,893.5	383.9	83.1
1974	5,365.7	429.1	92.6
1975	4,563.1	362.4	92.6
1976	6,321.6	429.5	93.6
1977	7,969.2	704.3	91.9
1978	5,400.6	662.8	88.0
1979	10,166.8	670.0	93.5
1980	13,523.0	554.0	96.0

Source: CBN, Extracted and computed from 'Nigeria's Imports and Exports', *Economic and Financial Review*, December, 1978, p. 14, and from *Annual Report and Statement of Accounts*, December, 1980, p. 89.

strong correlation between monetised foreign exchange of the Nigerian public sector and the money supply of the Nigerian economy.

4. Balance of Trade

Table 5.3 shows Nigeria's export statistics covering the period 1960-80. It speaks for itself. Between 1960 and 1968 non-oil exports contributed more to Nigeria's foreign exchange receipts, but between 1970 and 1980 oil has continued to dominate Nigeria's import and export statistics as the main foreign exchange earner of the country. By 1980 non-oil exports contributed to only 4 per cent of Nigeria's total export earnings as against 96 per cent of foreign exchange proceeds earned through oil exports.

Nigeria's balance of trade for non-oil items has been persistently on the deficit side since 1960. With the increase in foreign exchange earnings from oil exports, the monetisation of such earnings by the public sector also increased causing an expansion of Nigeria's domestic money income which generated a large demand for imports. The liberalisation of foreign exchange transactions and the relaxation of trade restrictions during the oil boom periods significantly increased the demand for imports. Non-oil export earnings became grossly inadequate to pay for the increase in the demand for imported capital and consumer goods. Oil exports have redeemed Nigeria's balance of payments account from what otherwise would have been a situation of persistent deficit had Nigeria depended on non-oil export earnings alone. Oil export has been a major contributor to the relatively favourable balance of payments and external reserves position of Nigeria.

5. Oil and Government Revenue

Government revenue in Nigeria is defined to mean the revenue of the Federal Government of Nigeria and those of the 19 state governments of Nigeria. The main sources of revenue for both federal and state governments are direct and indirect taxes. Under direct taxes are the following:

(1) Company Tax (including Supertax)

    (2) Personal Income Tax
    (3) Petroleum Profit Tax
    (4) Other Tax Revenue (Motor Vehicle Licences, Cattle Tax, Entertainment Tax and Sales/Purchase Taxes)

Indirect taxes constitute the following:

    (1) Import Duties
    (2) Export Duties
    (3) Excise Duties
    (4) Interest and Repayments
    (5) Mining (royalties, rents, fees, etc.)
    (6) Miscellaneous (earnings, savings, reimbursements and rent on government property, etc.)

The Federal Government collects such direct taxes as company tax, petroleum tax and other minor taxes grouped under 'Other Tax Revenue'. Indirect taxes which the Federal Government alone collects include import and export duties, excise duties and royalties, rents and fees resulting from mining activities as well as other miscellaneous indirect taxes assigned to it by law.

Of paramount interest here is the contribution of oil revenue to the overall revenue of the Federal Government which has the responsibility of reallocating it between the federal, state and local governments. Oil revenue accrues to the Federal Government from petroleum profit tax and mining (royalties, rents and fees). Another major source of government revenue especially with the changes in petroleum agreements between the government and the oil companies is the revenue from the direct marketing of government-owned shares of crude oil.

The major determinants of oil revenue include developments in the petroleum profit tax rates, the level of oil production which depends on the OPEC quota and the price of oil which again is determined by OPEC, the percentage of government equity participation in the oil industry, and the overall world market demand for oil which can influence world oil prices. The present oil glut is a case in point. With the formation of a Nigerian-owned oil company, the distribution and marketing of refined oil and allied products are carried out by the Nigerian National Petroleum Company. Additional revenue is now derived from the storage and sale of petroleum products including oil pipeline licences and survey fees.

Table 5.4: Current Revenue of the Federal Government, 1973-8 January-December (₦ million)

Type and Source	1973	1974	1975	1976	1977	1978
DIRECT TAXES	852.9	3,032.1	2,990.2	3,852.4	4,839.8	3,962.3
Personal Income Tax	75.5	146.1	261.9	222.2	476.9	3.3
Company Income Tax	1.2	11.1	15.9	3.5	3.3	527.4
Petroleum Profit Tax	769.2	2,872.5	2,707.5	3,624.9	4,330.8	3,415.7
Other Tax Revenue[a]	7.0	1.9	4.9	1.8	28.8	15.9
INDIRECT TAXES	516.2	498.2	760.7	882.7	1,145.6	1,698.2
Import Duties	307.9	328.3	629.3	724.3	964.2	1,436.2
Export Duties	12.3	5.5	5.8	6.1	4.2	2.8
Excise Duties	196.0	164.4	125.5	152.3	177.2	259.2
Interest and Repayments	49.8	127.1	162.7	189.0	266.1	523.6
Mining (Rent, Royalties Rent Fee) etc.	246.8	854.2	1,564.0	1,740.3	1,749.8	1,238.4
Miscellaneous[b]	29.6	25.4	37.1	101.5	41.1	46.8
TOTAL	1,695.3	4,537.0	5,514.7	6,765.9	8,042.4	7,469.3

Notes: a. Includes capital gains, casino and airport taxes.
b. Includes earnings and sales, fees and licences, reimbursement and other receipts also not elsewhere specified.

Source: CBN, *Economic and Financial Review*, December, 1979, p. 80.

Table 5.5: Trends in Petroleum Profit Tax Rates

From Inception	—	19 March 1971	50%
20 March 1971	—	30 September 1974	55%
1 October 1974	—	30 November 1974	60.78%
1 December 1974	—	31 March 1975	65.75%
1 April 1975	—	31 March 1977	85%

Source: NNPC, *NAPETCOR*, October–December, 1980, p. 7.

Table 5.4 shows the current revenue of the Federal Government from 1973 to 1978. One of the major sources of oil revenue for the Federal Government is revenue arising from marketing of government equity oil either directly or through third party agents. This is not reflected in Table 5.4. Since 1973 oil receipts have constituted the largest single source of revenue for the Federal Government.

The second major source of oil revenue is petroleum profit tax. The major determinants of the level of petroleum profit tax are the changes in the rate of petroleum profit tax, the level of demand for crude and, of course, the price of petroleum products. Until 1969, petroleum profit tax was statistically lumped under *Other Tax Revenue*. It was from 1970 that petroleum profit tax became separated and treated independently as its importance grew. Petroleum profit tax is still the largest single source of oil money for the government. Table 5.5 shows developments in the rate of petroleum profit tax in Nigeria between 1960 and 1977. The rates have changed over the years. From 50 per cent, which it was until 1971, it rose to 85 per cent between 1975 and 1977. Since 1977 the rate has virtually remained unchanged. There is no doubt that the increase in the rate of petroleum profit tax has invariably influenced the volume of petroleum profit tax over the years.

Royalties including rent and fees constitute the third source of oil revenue to the government. Royalty is calculated as a percentage of posted prices of oil as well as petroleum profit tax. Posted prices may not necessarily reflect actual market prices of the different blends of oil. They were arbitrarily determined for the purpose of calculating petroleum profit tax and royalty. In the early days of the oil industry such posted prices were determined by the oil companies themselves but with the equity participation of the Federal Government in the oil industry and in keeping with an OPEC resolution that member countries should have a greater say in their oil policies, NNPC now has a say in the determination of posted prices in conjunction with foreign oil partners.

When an oil company is granted a concession it starts paying rent on that concession. The rent will vary according to the area conceded to it. When an oil company starts production the payment of rent ceases and the total rent paid before production is translated into royalty. Hence the annual rent of an oil company is called advance royalty. The maximum number of years an oil company is allowed to pay rent is 20 years after which the mining lease terminates.

It seems that for some time to come the oil industry will continue to be the engine of the Nigerian economy. Experts are are of the opinion that when the LNG project becomes fully operational by 1990, gas may be another major source of revenue to the government and to the economy in general.

6. Manpower and Technology

Expectations are high that the oil industry will provide a stepping stone for the acquisition of the practical manpower and technological transfers which Nigeria requires for her industrial development pro-grammes. The oil industry provides forward and backward linkage effects for any economy. It creates other industries such as petro-chemical and fertiliser industries. Among Nigerian industries the oil industry has the largest number of trained manpower in engineering and management. It is hoped that some of these highly trained managers and engineers will eventually filter into other areas of industrial activity to form the nucleus of further manpower develop-ments.

7. External Debt

A country incurs external debt through a number of ways such as contractor finance, supplier credit, guaranteed private investment, loans from international financial markets, from international organisations such as the World Bank (IBRD) and its agencies the International Monetary Fund (IMF), intergovernmental loans, multilateral private loans such as those from the Eurocurrency markets.

Loans are of three types — long-term loans, medium-term loans and short-term loans, the last type consisting mainly of trade credit, while long- and medium-term loans are in most cases designated for development projects.

Many factors determine the nature and level of external debt a country can incur. These include the balance of payments position, the external reserve level, debt and the ability of the public and private sectors of the economy to generate revenue from domestic sources. Where the private, or the public sector, is unable to raise revenue from domestic sources it may be compelled to seek external loans which will be monetised into local currency for the purpose of executing the proposed project or projects. However, if the project has a very high foreign exchange cost-content such cost can only be met through foreign exchange earnings from exports or through grants or external borrowings. Any country which embarks upon programmes with a high foreign exchange cost-content will invariably have a difficult time especially during the debt-service payments period, i.e. payments of interest charges and amortisation. A country which borrows foreign exchange to meet today's needs is expected to earn adequate foreign exchange in the future to meet debt obligations when due.

(a) Nigeria's Outstanding External Debts

Table 5.6 shows the outstanding debts of Nigeria. Most of Nigeria's external debts are of the long- and medium-term types. Medium-

Table 5.6: Federal Public External Debt Outstanding

Year	Amount (₦ million)	Year	Amount (₦ million)
1960	82.4	1971	214.5
1961	85.8	1972	263.5
1962	140.8	1973	276.9
1963	181.4	1974	322.4
1964	365.6	1975	349.9
1965	435.2	1976	374.6
1966	438.6	1977	373.1
1967	430.4	1978	1,252.1
1968	426.0	1979	1,611.5
1969	456.0	1980	1,866.8
1970	488.8		

Source: CBN, *Economic and Financial Review,* and *Annual Report and Statement of Accounts* (various issues).

term debts were incurred during the period from 1964 to 1966 when Nigeria's balance of payments position was very poor, and between 1967 and 1970 during the civil war years, when Nigeria required additional foreign exchange for the purchase of arms for the war effort and other essential items.

All external debts are guaranteed by the Federal Government of Nigeria. The Federal Government guarantees the foreign debts it contracts as well as those of the state governments, local governments and government agencies, public corporations and, in special cases, private investment. The capacity of Nigeria to settle her foreign debt obligations largely depends on the proceeds earned through oil exports.

(b) Factors Which Influence Nigeria's External Debt Level

Any country wishing to borrow from domestic or external sources and to repay the debt promptly at a future date has to take into account the probable level of domestic revenue, the projected foreign exchange earnings through exports of goods and services, and the projected imports as well as the expected level of recurrent and capital expenditures. Where a country is able to raise revenue from domestic sources for capital and recurrent expenditure it may only need to borrow from external sources for prosecuting programmes with foreign exchange contents. If a country's capacity to export is high it may or may not have to borrow from external sources as the foreign exchange earnings may be adequate for the foreign exchange content programmes in the country's development plan.

The First and Second Development Plans of Nigeria were not as ambitious as the Third and Fourth Development plans. The First Plan of Nigeria which spanned the period between 1962 and 1968 expected about 41 per cent of the public sector investment, which totalled ₦653 million, to be financed from outside while the second plan envisaged 19.4 per cent foreign financing for the public sector. The Third Plan (1975 to 1980) and the Fourth Plan (1981 to 1985) envisage limited foreign financing for the public sector. It was hoped that Nigeria's oil money would provide any foreign exchange which the last two plans may require through the monetisation of foreign receipts, should revenue projections fall short of expected domestic expenditures. The Fourth Plan which has been revised a number of times was estimated to cost about ₦28 billion. The cost has since trebled because of worldwide inflation. Nigeria relied mainly on oil money for the plan's implementation. Unfortunately Nigeria miscalculated. An unexpected slump in the oil business began in 1977. Nigeria was forced to look for external loans if the development plans were to be completed successfully. In 1978, the then military government issued a decree which allowed Nigeria to incur foreign debt up to ₦5 billion. The total borrowing envisaged by Nigeria for the Fourth National Development Plan from both external and domestic sources was estimated at about ₦16.9 billion. A large portion of the amount was expected to be raised from external sources as the domestic finance market is grossly inadequate for raising such a large amount of money. The estimated total debt of the Fourth National Development Plan was based on the assumption that Nigeria will continue to produce 2.1 billion barrels of oil a day and at the selling price of about 36 dollars per barrel.

As far back as the 1977/8 fiscal year, Nigeria raised a loan total of $1.75 billion from the Eurocurrency market. Between 1979 and 1980 Nigeria is said to have raised another $2.8 billion dollars loan and in 1981 another loan of $2.2 million was also raised for the Ajokuta integrated steel mill. Estimated total foreign borrowing of Nigeria for 1981 was $5 billion.

All the loans were raised at exorbitant rates because of Nigeria's inexperience in international borrowing, and because of her less than impeccable record in the management of international loans in the past. The interest rates charged on those loans were over the London interbank office rate (LIBOR) and the fees charged were in excess of what is reasonable. In some cases the fees ranged between 2 to 3 per cent. The high cost of variable charges for Nigeria's loans have been attributed to her low rating in loan management in spite of her low debt services/gross national product ratio which is about 4 per cent and her debt service/current account ratio which is as low as 1.4 per cent. Nigeria uses third party bank negotiators who match borrower and lender and agency banks, the latter charging agency fees, management fees, legal fees, placement fees and commitment fees. These fees enlarge Nigeria's debt-service charges and make future payments extremely difficult. In the 1960s and 1970s Nigeria preferred the use of bilateral and multilateral intergovernmental loans which did not generate such variable charges as those enumerated above. The use of private sources such as the Eurocurrency market will cost Nigeria much more when the contracted loans mature, and the hope placed on the oil money is fading because of the world oil glut.

8. International Reserves

Table 5.7 shows the development in the external reserves of Nigeria from 1960, the year Nigeria gained political independence, to 1980. Until the 1970s agricultural commodities were the main foreign exchange earner for Nigeria. From 1967 to 1972 Nigeria's foreign external reserve levels dropped below the amount required for sustaining four months critical imports as shown in column three of the Table. From 1973, however, Nigeria's external reserves rose dramatically as a result of the increase in oil prices occasioned by the Arab oil embargo on the Western countries for alleged complicity in the 1973 Yom Kippur War in which the Arab countries bordering Israel sustained heavy losses in material, men and land. The Arab use of oil as a political weapon sharply increased oil prices and sky-rocketted Nigeria's external reserves in 1975 to a record level, to such

Table 5.7: External Reserves in ₦ Million

Year ended	Level of Reserves ₦ million	Import Adequacy in Months
1960	343.3	9.5
1961	305.5	8.2
1962	250.6	7.4
1963	192.4	5.6
1964	193.5	4.6
1965	197.2	4.3
1966	184.60	4.3
1967	102.2	2.7
1968	105.3	3.3
1969	114.5	2.8
1970	180.4	2.9
1971	302.7	3.4
1972	273.3	3.3
1973	438.4	4.3
1974	3,540.9	24.4
1975	3,702.7	11.9
1976	3,481.6	9.8
1977	3,034.3	n.a.
1978	1,349.3	n.a.
1979	3,250.8	n.a.
1980	5,648.2	n.a.

Source: S.B. Falegan, *Management of Nigeria's External Reserves*, NIIA, Lagos, 1978 and Central Bank of Nigeria Publications.

an extent that Nigeria could have afforded to import goods and services for up to 24.4 months without a single export, at the then current rate of import. But the new fortune of Nigeria was a transient business. As a result of precautionary measures taken by the major oil consuming nations of the West, oil glut set in and Nigeria had to fall back on her reserves which were virtually depleted by the early part of 1982.

The industrialised countries also reacted in another way. Prices of export commodities, as well as freight charges, were increased by the industrialised countries (to recover, amongst other things, the huge costs resulting from ever-increasing oil prices) with the consequence of worldwide inflation. Even though Nigeria's external reserve level increased in 1975, over and above what it was in 1974, the import adequacy of reserves measured in months declined to 11.9 months, a figure less than half the level of 1974. Although oil production increased in 1976 over and above what it was in 1975, the external reserve level of Nigeria declined in 1976 to 9.8 months. Nigeria began to experience financial difficulties because of this sudden twist in world oil demand, a circumstance which had an unfavourable effect on Nigeria's reserve position.

9. A Critical Review of Nigeria's External Reserve Policy

Nigerian policy makers have been accused of both an injudicious use of Nigeria's external reserves and a lack of foresight in the anticipation of reserve levels. Nigerian critics argue that Nigeria has no long-term reserve policy. There is no external target for the country and there are no plans for realising any reserve target. External reserve levels realise themselves somewhat accidentally, as was the case in 1974, rather than through deliberate policy. There are no plans on how best to invest external reserves more productively. Instead of co-ordinated reserve plans Nigeria engages in the annual review of the balance of payments position to determine whether to liberalise or restrict imports and whether to increase or reduce travelling allowances, etc. If the external reserve level of Nigeria shows some signs of strain, Nigerian authorities immediately embark on panic monetary, fiscal and other economic intervention measures in an effort to correct the situation and stabilise reserve levels. Monetary and fiscal policies are juggled in the hope of correcting the situation but quite often the unco-ordinated measures only succeed in aggravating the situation. Nigeria's approach to the balance of payments problem has been criticised as grossly inadequate for a fast growingly economy.

The lack of an external reserve policy manifested itself in 1974, when Nigeria's external reserves level reached a record height. The Nigerian authorities were at a loss to know what to do with the huge external reserves which were wholly unanticipated. Because of the lack of a planned external reserve policy (targets and usage) the huge reserves could not be properly invested. The world monetary crisis and the regime of floating currencies made both the dollar and sterling assets most unsafe for investment purposes. As far back as 1974, the UK had withdrawn from the Sterling Guarantee Agreement (SGA) reached between Nigeria and the UK in 1968, whereby Nigeria was obliged to continue to keep the bulk of her assets in sterling. The UK was bound by the agreement to compensate Nigeria adequately for any loss sustained as a result of depreciation in value arising from any devaluation of sterling or any form of world monetary crisis which adversely affected the value of sterling. In 1974, the very year in which Nigeria had her record reserve level, the UK withdrew from the agreement in the wake of the regime of floating currencies. The value of Nigeria's external reserves began to depreciate as sterling fluctuated sharply on the foreign exchange market.

By mid-1975 Nigeria was forced to set up an *Investment Management Committee* headed by the deputy governor of the Central Bank and other senior officials of the bank. The committee was given a mandate to study the world monetary situation and to take the necessary steps to diversify Nigeria's external reserves in the assets of other countries — taking into consideration acceptability, quicker monetisation of the assets and the degree of stability of the asset. From traditional sterling assets Nigeria diversified her external reserves into US dollars, Deutsche marks, Swiss francs, French francs, Canadian dollars, Japanese yen, SDR and gold assets. The Deutsche mark was the strongest of all the assets but the West German authorities were reluctant to allow their vehicle currency to be used as a 'hide out' for Nigerian oil money. Instead of earning interest, Nigerian deposit accounts with German banks attracted negative interest rates which tended to wipe out efforts to compensate Nigeria's weaker external assets with the gains from the stronger Deutsche mark. It is not quite positive that Nigeria achieved the desired objective which was intended throughout to balance out losses sustained from weaker currencies by the yields from the more stable currencies such as the

German mark, the Swiss franc and the Japanese yen.

The Investment Management Committee (IMC) of 1975 was a short-term crises committee as its terms of reference suggested. What Nigeria needed is an enlarged committee on a permanent basis, to plan Nigeria's external reserve levels and the usage of such reserves, taking into account the present and projected future world economic situations. In this exercise, the variables and parameters of the economy have to be kept in mind in order to arrive at balanced conclusions.

In planning options, Nigeria's development programmes also have to be taken into consideration. Established projects and other activities have to be graded in order to eliminate non-priority projects or to slow them down depending on the reserve management option adopted. The projected reserve levels should determine the options to be employed for the management and usage of a country's reserves. In 1974, when the avalanche of reserves took place, Nigeria had no policy on how best to apply that part of the reserves in excess of that required for satisfying four months critical imports. The explosive reserve situation occurred just at the beginning of Nigeria's Third National Development Plan period (1975 to 1980). The excess reserves which were invested in the asset portfolio of other countries should have been used to support the Third National Development Plan which contained a number of projects with high foreign exchange content. By investing in the assets of other countries, Nigeria increases the productivity and employment levels of other countries at the expense of Nigeria's own economic development.

10. Other Economic Blunders in the 1970s

The 1970s were characterised by a number of economic blunders. The year 1973 witnessed the devaluation of the naira contrary to expert advice. The Bretton Woods Agreement of 1945 which determined the exchange rate between international currencies allowed for a narrow fluctuation band. By 1970 the band had become too tight. In 1971 the restrictive Bretton Woods 'band' was ripped open by the tense world monetary situation. An agreement was reached between the USA and other key currency countries which culminated in the Smithsonian Agreement with a 4.5 per cent fluctuation band. As a result of the Smithsonian Agreement, the US severed the links between the dollar and gold. The semi-automatic link between the dollar and gold had made the US dollar the king of reserve currencies and the most preferred vehicle currency for international trade. The absence of the gold-dollar link reduced the dollar bill to the same level of consideration and preference as other international vehicle currencies. Shortly after the dollar began to float and the world monetary crisis deepened. This was aggravated by the noncommittal position of the US in defending the value of the dollar in terms of the Smithsonian Agreement. Consequently the value of the dollar depreciated beyond the lower margin of the band. The situation was worsened by the rumour of an agreement between EEC countries to establish an exchange rate band of not more than 2.5 per cent on either side of par and allow their currencies to float against non-EEC currencies if necessary. This is the so called *snake in the tunnel* agreement. The speculation of an impending agreement caused a further fall in the dollar exchange rate. The Smithsonian band became too tight in the course of time and was discarded. The free float began.

In 1973 the US dollar was devalued. Nigeria followed the US example by devaluing the naira. According to Nigerian authorities it was in Nigeria's interests to realign the naira value to a key currency, such as the dollar. But by devaluing her currency Nigeria unwittingly triggered off a domestic monetary crisis. Import prices rose as well as domestic market prices. Speculation was rife that there were to be further rises in prices. There was therefore a stampede by businessmen to increase imports. Nigerian traders began to hoard imported goods already in stock. Demand for imported goods could not be met as devaluation did not in any way increase Nigeria's exports and foreign exchange earnings because of the inelasticity of Nigeria's export products and the cartel-tied prices of others (for example, crude oil, groundnuts and cocoa). If the export products of a country are elastic, devaluation alters the exchange rate between the devaluing currency and those of the rest of the world which did not devalue. The export prices of the devaluing country become cheaper and more competitive in the international market. Only countries which produce and export consumer and capital goods such as electronic goods, industrial plant and machinery, vehicles, refrigerators, equipment and tools benefit from devaluation. Devaluation does not favour countries which produce primary products such as cocoa, groundnuts and palm produce. These are Nigeria's major export products and they are inelastic with respect to prices and demand. Devaluation did not help Nigeria and cannot do so in the foreseeable future. Obviously the devaluation of 1973 was a mistake and it may have contributed in a significant way to Nigeria's present economic ills.

At the time Nigeria was devaluing her currency, efforts were being made to increase wages and salaries. If devaluation is to succeed it must be backed by a freeze on wages, salaries and prices. The contrary was the case in Nigeria. The Udoji Salaries and Wages Review Commission was set up; it drastically increased salaries of workers especially the salaries of those who were already in high income brackets. In some cases salaries were doubled. The consequence was an increase in the demand for imports when the awards were made in 1975. It is no wonder that within a year of the Udoji salary awards Nigeria's reserve levels took a deep plunge from 24.4 months import equivalent in 1974 to 11.9 in 1975 and 9.8 in 1976. The import equivalent level of reserves has continued to decline since then. By the early part of 1982 Nigeria hardly had enough reserves to sustain two months imports.

The discovery of oil gave rise emotions of pride and joy in terms of what the discovery meant to the health and development of the Nigerian economy. But it led the country into false expectations, unco-ordinated planning, staggering projects, false expenditure and miscalculation. The boom has turned into doom especially in the 1980s.

It is true that the only Nigerian product which contributes almost 90 per cent of Nigeria's national income and foreign exchange, and about 85 per cent of Nigeria's government revenue, is crude oil. It is the only Nigerian product which in the absence of a cartel agreement is elastic in price on the international market. But Nigeria cannot influence the export of oil alone because Nigeria is a member of the OPC Cartel which establishes quota and market prices for the various blends of oil of member countries. It was not through the devaluation exercise of 1973 that Nigeria increased her oil exports in 1974 and accumulated a record reserve of 24.4 months import equivalent. The increase in 1973 of Nigeria's oil exports has already beenn explained as being due to the Arab oil boycott of 1973. In Nigeria's circumstances devaluation cannot promote exports. It may deter imports, if import restrictions are backed by austerity measures. Proponents of devaluation argue that the naira was overvalued in 1973 and that non-devaluation would imply subsidising imports. The argument is weak. There are other ways of offsetting such a subsidy without endangering the economy. Drastic import and tariff masures can wipe out the subsidy effects on imports arising from the non-devaluation of overvalued currency without causing any panic or speculation of the kind which devaluation brings to an economy.

References and Additional Reading

'Federal Government To Reactivate Enugu Coal Mine', in the *Business Times*, Lagos, Nigeria, 17 May 1982
'LNG Project Will Cost More With Delays', in the *Punch*, Lagos, Nigeria, 18 May 1982
'Nigeria and the Oil Market', in the *National Concord*, Lagos, Nigeria, 14 April 1982
'Nigeria's Oil Revenue Falling', in the *Sunday Tribune*, Ibadan, Nigeria, 16 Aug. 1981
'Oil Production Drop: Is it a Conspiracy?', in the *Business Times*, Lagos, Nigeria, 19 April 1982
Oil and Gas Journal, Petroleum Publishing Company, Tulsa, Oklahoma, (weekly)
Okeke, E.I., 'Oil in the Nigerian Economy', in *NAPETCOR*, vol. 1, no. 1, Oct.-Dec., 1980
Okeke, E.I., 'Oil in Nigerian Economy', in *NAPETCOR*, Quarterly Magazine of The Nigerian National Petroleum Company, vol. 2, no. 2, April-June, 1981
Onoh, J.K., *Strategic Approaches To Crucial Policies in Economic Development*, Rotterdam University Press, Rotterdam, 1972
Onoh, J.K., (Ed.) *The Foundations of Nigeria's Financial Infrastructure*, Croom Helm, London, 1981
Ozumba, C.C., 'Dollar Depreciation — Effect on Purchasing Power of Nigerian Oil', in *NAPETCOR*, vol. 2, no. 1, Jan.-March, 1981
'Private Jetties and the Economy', in the *Daily Times*, Lagos, Nigeria, 26 April 1982
'The Economy and Nigerians', in the *Daily Times*, Lagos, Nigeria, 24 April 1982
'The Faltering Boom — Implies Bleak Economic Prospect', in the *Financial Punch*, Lagos, Nigeria, 29 March 1982
'The Ups and Downs of Nigeria's Oil Fortune', in the *Daily Times*, Lagos, Nigeria, 29 March 1982

6 NIGERIA'S OIL CRISIS IN THE EARLY 1980s

Both endogenous and exogenous factors have contributed to Nigeria's present economic crisis. The endogenous factor is Nigeria's inability to plan her own resources. The exogeneous factors include the conservation measures of the industrialised countries, the tactics of the international oil conglomerates, the Saudi factor in OPEC and the roles of the non-OPEC oil producing countries whose oil output has significantly increased over the years and whose pricing tactics are threatening the long-standing oil price monopoly of OPEC. This inability to plan resources was discussed in Chapter six. This chapter will therefore mainly consider the exogenous factors which have adverse effects on Nigeria's oil production output and income. It will also discuss the austerity measures taken by the Nigerian authorities to contain the ominous trends in her economy.

1. Conservation Measures of the Industrialised Countries

When the price of oil rose in 1973 the industrialised world was shocked. The belief was general that the situation was a temporary one, but OPEC member nations contrary to belief continued to increase oil prices. They argued that the increase in oil prices would offset the increase in the prices of imported goods from the industrialised countries. The Western countries soon realised that the era of cheap energy was gone as oil price per barrel rose from a little below $3.4 in 1973 to about $41 per barrel by December, 1981. The price of $41 per barrel implied an increase of 150 per cent between mid-1980 and December 1981. The industrialised countries foresaw untold hardships for their economies, such as the bankruptcy of firms, unemployment and recession should definite steps not be taken to counter rising oil prices. To forestall any crisis the industrialised countries teamed together to devise measures for conserving oil and other energies which they depended on the developing countries to supply. In February, 1974 the World Energy Conference organised by the industrialised countries met to discuss a sharing formula in the event of a crisis. The result was the formation of the Energy Co-ordinating Group which met in Brussels in July, 1974 and reached 'substantial agreement' on the scheme according to the official communiqué. As a follow-up the United States, West Germany, the United Kingdom and Japan met in Tokyo in 1976 and formed the International Energy Agency (IEA). The objective of the agency was to devise means of conserving energy in order to frustrate the oil pricing policy of OPEC, while researching alternative sources of energy which before the turn of the century are expected to make the industrialised countries less dependent on oil. The member nations have contributed large amounts of money in order to realise this objective.

The International Energy Agency has drawn up a number of programmes on energy conservation and is experimenting with alternative sources of energy. Politically, the member nations of the IEA are very active and are using the non-OPEC oil producing countries as well as some members of OPEC, especially Saudi Arabia, to achieve a reduction in oil prices. The International Energy Agency is expected to reduce the oil consumption of the industrialised countries through immediate conservation measures by 10 per cent or the equivalent of 4.1 million barrels per day. Traditional sources of energy such as coal have been drawn back into use. Some major industries which depend largely on crude oil are being remodelled to utilise coal, and efforts are being made to gasify coal as well. Industries and domestic consumers have been advised to be judicious in the use of oil as a short-term measure. Motorists have been urged to reduce speed in order to reduce fuel consumption. People have been advised to switch off heaters in their homes, especially when they are away from home and to reduce the use of neon lights for advertisements. These immediate short-term measures have contributed significantly to a reduction in oil bills for the industrialised countries.

In addition to the utilisation of coal and coal gasification, the industrialised countries are experimenting on other long-term alternative sources of energy. Coal is also being refined to produce oil although at great cost. Refuse, maize and sugar cane are now potential raw materials for the production of oil. Research on the conversion of ocean waves into energy for the purpose of electrification is being intensively carried out. Electrical energy so converted will be carried over long distances and finally distributed through cables to industries and homes. Solar energy is also undergoing experimentation and the use of nuclear energy for industrial purposes has reached an advanced stage. If the experiments are successful they will offer the industrialised countries the cheapest form of power to industries and homes. Then the industrialised countries will have acquired very important weapons which will be more reliable and more effective for disorganising OPEC than the use of non-OPEC members and some OPEC members to achieve a drastic reduction in oil prices and to herald once more a new era of cheap energy.

2. The Tactics of the Oil Conglomerates

The international oil conglomerates or the big seven are: British Petroleum, Exxon Corporation, Gulf Corporation, Mobil Oil Corporation, Royal Dutch Shell Group, Standard Oil Company of California and Texaco Incorporated. These companies are not only oil exploration companies: their activities are neatly inter-woven with the policies of their home governments. They are required as a matter of national policy to obtain as cheaply as possible strategic raw materials (oil) for sustaining home industries in order to maintain full employment and rapid economic growth. The oil multinationals constitute an integral part of the inter-national instruments of Western countries for achieving the policy of cheap strategic raw materials.

The formation of OPEC in September, 1960 was a protest against these oil companies who alone determined what price they would pay for a barrel of crude oil. The seven multinational oil companies monopolised the entire world oil business, determined the quantity of oil to be produced and also the prices to be paid to the oil producing countries. In the early period of the operation of these companies poor rent and royalties were paid and oil produc-ing countries were not allowed to participate in the production or sale of the oil.

Towards the end of 1959 a new constellation started to form. Oil multinationals continued unilaterally to reduce crude oil prices without any consultation whatsoever with the oil producing coun-tries. Thus in 1959, the Venezuelan posted oil price was reduced to about $0.25 per barrel and in the Middle East the average posted price per barrel was $0.18. While the major oil producing countries such as Venezuela, Iran, Iraq, Kuwait and Saudi Arabia were incensed by the reduction of 1959, the Middle East oil price was reduced further to 14 cents per barrel. Because of these continuous reductions in the price of crude oil, the five major oil producing countries named above decided in 1960 to form OPEC (Organisation of Petroleum-Exporting Countries) in order to participate both in oil production policy and in oil price policy in the interests of their own economies. Since 1960 the oil multinationals have been on a head-on collision course with the major oil producing countries. Attempts are being made to destroy the monopoly of OPEC and to force oil prices to follow the natural law of supply and demand. Every effort is being made by the oil multinationals to destabilise OPEC directly and indirectly. The present oil crisis resulting from an oil glut is suspected by the oil producing countries to be a long-term strategy and tactic of the oil multinationals for achieving a three-point strategy:

(1) To overproduce and make the supply of oil outstrip the demand for oil thereby causing a fall in world oil prices;

(2) To persuade non-OPEC oil producing countries to step up their production for the same purpose of causing an excess supply of oil in the world market in order to bring down oil prices or, alternatively to bring pressure to bear on non-OPEC oil producing countries to reduce their oil prices and thereby jeopardise OPEC's own reference price;

(3) To destabilise OPEC by playing OPEC member countries one against the other or by using the services of their governments to influence key OPEC policies such as oil production and pricing.

The long-term strategy of the multinationals yielded some dividends for them in the late 1970s and early 1980s culminating in the world oil glut which threw the entire OPEC policy out of phase and nearly caused a disintegration of OPEC as a functioning organisation.

Since 1977 the oil companies have stepped up their tactics and have been involved in a number of speculative oil purchases especially on the spot market. Although speculative purchases pushed up oil prices to about $41 per barrel by December 1981 it was only a temporary boom for the oil producing countries because the long-term objective was to achieve a cut in OPEC oil prices. The oil companies had stockpiled oil to last over 100 days by December, 1981. The strategy was to decline to purchase some blends of OPEC oil until they conformed with the prices of non-OPEC oil producing countries. This policy of the multinationals affected Nigeria's oil production very severely as Nigeria produces the same blend of oil as the British National Oil Corporation (BNOC).

The timing of the crisis was excellent because Nigeria, a member of OPEC had at the time an external reserve level which was grossly inadequate for supporting even two months imports. Nigeria was forced to the wall and it was expected that Nigeria would pull out from OPEC and sell her oil at a market determined price as that provided the only realistic avenue for salvaging her economy from destruction. In the early part of 1982 the international oil companies were accused of concentrating their tactics on Nigeria — the weakest link in the OPEC chain. The oil companies were alleged to have refused to lift Nigerian oil on the pretext that prices for Nigerian blends did not correspond with the prices of equivalent blends from other oil producing countries especially with that of BNOC, whose blends are of the same quality as those of Nigeria. While Nigeria's oil sold at $35.05 per barrel, that of BNOC sold for $31 per barrel. The oil companies have vigorously defended themselves: as profit-making ventures they argue that shareholders will not listen to excuses for losses; hence they had to cut back their Nigerian oil production in order to reduce costs. High operating and production costs cut drastically into their profit margins. Instead of 80 cents profit per barrel they were said to hardly make 20 cents per barrel because the oil companies do not only produce for exports but also for domestic demand and the domestic prices of oil products are relatively lower in Nigeria than in other countries. Additionally the oil companies argued that tax rates are too high in Nigeria and depress oil profits.

Spokesmen of the Nigerian based oil companies contend that the oil companies had continued to lift oil from Nigeria contrary to reports but that NNPC, Nigeria's joint venture partner with the oil companies, has been unable to sell its share of oil because it deals through third party agents who number 34. These third party agents have been described as 'purely traders and birds of passage'. They are not so committed as the oil companies. They appear in good business seasons and disappear in bad seasons. They purchase oil when oil prices are lucrative and disappear when prices of oil experience slump. However, there may be more than a grain of truth in the accusations of the oil companies about the mode of operation of third party agents. During the Crude Oil Sales Scandal Tribunal, third party agents featured in a very bad light. Some were accused of lifting oil but never actually paying for it. It is known that the most lucrative form of political patronage in Nigeria is the granting of a third party oil agency to political 'big guns'. Some of these agents do not have any experience in the oil business. They in turn have to look out for other agents who may turn out to be international crooks.

Nigeria was accused of being unrealistic by expecting between 2.1 to 2.3 million barrels of oil per day to be produced in the face of an oil glut. A realistic figure for Nigeria should have been between 900,000 barrels to 1.3 million barrels per day. The Shell Oil Development Company, for example, argued that it honoured its own obligation by taking its full oil share corresponding to its 20 per cent equity holding of its oil capital investment in Nigeria and in addition it purchased an additional 100,000 barrels per day from the NNPC's own share of oil.

In the wake of the Nigerian oil crisis there was widespread fear among OPEC members that Nigeria might opt out of OPEC and sell her crudes on the open market at a price which would cut OPEC's own reference prices drastically. Nigeria's revised Development Plan was estimated at over ₦80 billion. While Nigeria's imports averaged 1.8 billion dollars a month, Nigeria's reserves were estimated in the early part of 1982 at only ₦3 billion. If Nigeria's development programmes were to be executed and if imports were to be maintained Nigeria needed more money and quickly. Nigeria was therefore under pressure at home to opt out of OPEC and to sell her crudes on the open market in order to acquire the foreign exchange required for sustaining her developmental programmes, for supporting imports and for honouring international obligations including debt servicing. The other option for Nigeria was to borrow from the international money and capital market. But Nigeria's credit rating is very low in spite of her oil wealth, and borrowing could be difficult in the circumstance. Again, because of high interest rates in the region of 22 per cent in the US and over 12 per cent in the Eurocurrency market, and the exorbitant legal and placement fees, borrowing was considered a non-starter for Nigeria. It was feared that Nigeria would opt out of OPEC and if that happened OPEC as an organisation would disintegrate. OPEC members were alarmed. Saudi Arabia promised $1 billion in credit and the Saudi oil minister, Sheik Ahmed Zaki

Yamani warned, in the wake of the crisis, that companies which took advantage of Nigeria's vulnerability and reduced its lifting of Nigeria's crude would be punished by OPEC. Saudi Arabia promised to cut down on any additional oil production in order to tighten the market and keep prices steady. Nigeria and Venezuela were expected to benefit from the Saudi production cut by raising their production levels a little to ease the tight situations in which they found themselves.

3. The Saudi Arabian Factor

Ironically, Saudi Arabia which was apparently concerned with Nigeria's economic plight was responsible for creating the oil glut. Saudi Arabia, a founder member of OPEC, produces about 41 per cent of OPEC's total oil output. By maintaining a high production level of 10.3 million barrels per day in spite of the world oil supply pressure, Saudi Arabia caused a situation which helped the industrialised nations to consolidate and stockpile oil which they later pushed onto the spot market to flood the oil market and push down spot market prices of oil. Saudi Arabia has always professed friendship with the industrialised countries and very often went along with their biddings. Saudi Arabia was persuaded by the industrialised countries of the West to step up her oil production in order to fill the gap in supply created by the Iran/Iraq war. Iran and Iraq were forced by circumstances to sell as much as they could produce at prices below OPEC's reference prices in order to acquire the much needed foreign exchange for purchasing war armaments. The Iranian and Iraqi oil sales also helped to cause the glut as it was not possible to estimate the actual shortage of oil in the world market caused by the Iran/Iraqi war. It is believed by analysts that Western oil consumers overestimated the gap in the quantities of oil which Iraq and Iran should have supplied to the world oil market under normal circumstances. Saudi Arabia, which was persuaded to produce the shortage, was in actual fact producing a surplus which was far in excess of the shortage caused by the Iran/Iraq war.

Before Saudi Arabia was able to discover that it was being used by the industrialised countries as an instrument for achieving a situation of oil glut and to destroy OPEC solidarity the damage had been done. Saudi Arabia realised rather late in the day that the industrialised world was also urging the non-OPEC oil producing countries to step up their production in order to destroy OPEC's calculated production level and force down OPEC's oil price. The Saudi Oil Minister was angry when he discovered the strategy of the major oil consuming countries. However he defended the Saudi policy of price stabilisation through slightly increased production. Saudi Arabia argued that oil prices could only be stabilised if they were first reduced. The Saudi Oil Minister considered the price of $41 per barrel as rather too high and likely to cause recession. He vowed that his country would flood the market with more oil if need be until the 13 member nations of OPEC agreed to a price reduction. He attributed the worldwide recession to high oil prices.

The long-term strategy which he believed would protect the interests of OPEC members would be to reduce oil prices and stabilise them at a certain level. If stabilised oil prices are achieved, Saudi Arabia argued, then the price of oil would then be pegged to the rate of inflation and the real economic growth rate of the industrialised countries of the West who are OPEC's main customers. The Western argument, as the hawkish members of OPEC dubbed the Saudi proposal, was most unacceptable. At the OPEC meeting held in the early part of 1982 at Vienna and Geneva the member nations of OPEC were in disarray as to the proper policy to pursue. In a subsequent meeting at Quito in Equador an agreement was reached on production cutbacks in a bid to defend OPEC's reference prices. Quotas were assigned to member nations which were to be religiously adhered to. Saudi Arabia has now realised that it can no longer set the pace on oil policy for OPEC as it did before, a course which the other member countries were bound to follow. Considering the increasing role of non-OPEC oil producing countries in the world oil market, OPEC member nations including Saudi Arabia have to stick together or perish, if the open-ended, *laisser-faire* policy of 'Do It Yourself' is to be allowed.

4. The Roles of the Non-OPEC Oil Producing Countries

The roles of the oil producing companies of non-OPEC countries such as the UK, Norway, Mexico and Egypt helped to worsen the world oil crisis and to destabilise OPEC's oil strategy. The non-OPEC oil producing countries in the past aligned their oil prices to the reference prices of OPEC. But since the beginning of 1982 non-

OPEC oil producing countries no longer align their prices to that of OPEC. It is believed by OPEC member countries that non-OPEC members are under political pressure from the industrialised countries of the West to cut their oil prices in order to influence OPEC's own reference prices. The price of British North Sea oil, which is of the same quality as that of Nigeria, was reduced, in spite of the high cost of BNOC production, from $36.5 per barrel to $31 per barrel in February 1982, while Nigeria's oil sold at $35.50 per barrel. The price slash by BNOC also put OPEC's reference price of $34.00 per barrel out of balance. Nigeria was hurt most by BNOC's action. Analysts believe that the nationalisation by Nigeria of British Petroleum interests during the critical period of negotiation for Zimbabwe's independence motivated BNOC's price cut. By that action Nigeria attempted to twist the arms of Mrs Thatcher's Government and force the UK government into a speedier negotiation on majority rule for Zimbabwe. The nationalisation of British Petroleum interests in Nigeria was followed by further veiled threats to nationalise British multibillion naira interests in Nigeria, if the UK government failed to force a quick decision on majority rule in Zimbabwe. The loss of British interests in Nigeria could not have been so easily forgotten. While helping the industrialised countries of the West of which the UK is a member by providing cheap oil, Britain, it is alleged, also intended a political vendetta against Nigeria by synchronising the oil price-cut to agree with the time when Nigeria's foreign reserve position was at its all time lowest. To Nigerian analysts, to hurt Nigeria was more important, otherwise the British Government would not have volunteered to lose a revenue of nearly £51 billion (unless, of course, it wished to make BNOC oil prices more competitive) by reducing North Sea oil prices by $4 and maintaining a wide output level of 1.9 million barrels per day, and this in the wake of the Falkland Islands conflict with Argentina. The estimated cost of production of North Sea oil is $29 per barrel while the market price was set at only $31 per barrel. Other informed circles are of the opinion that the industrialised countries agreed to write off British losses in order to achieve the long-term objective of crippling OPEC's oil price leadership and forcing oil prices to be determined by the market forces of supply and demand, which if allowed would reduce oil prices per barrel to an average of about $24 within a short time.

Although the strategy has not worked out as expected there was no doubt in the minds of OPEC members and non-OPEC members that things could no longer be the same any more. OPEC and non-OPEC future oil price strategies would have to take cognisance of the stark realities of world power politics. The only instrument available to Third World countries for counterbalancing the international political 'menaces' of the big powers has been shaken to its foundations.

5. The Consequences of the Oil Crisis on the Nigerian Economy

Nigeria experienced the first shock of oil glut during the 1977/8 financial year. By August, 1981 oil production had dropped from an average of 2.2 million barrels per day to 708,000 barrels per day. Apart from January, 1981 when the production level reached 2.1 million barrels per day, Nigeria had not been able subsequently to achieve that target level. The Fourth Development Plan which is

Table 6.1: OPEC Member Countries' Average Production in the Last Ten Yeaars and the New OPEC Level of Daily Production Quotas (Early 1982)

Country	(1) Average production in the last ten years ('000 b/d)	(2) Share	(3) New allocation ('000 b/d)	(4) (3/1) %
Algeria	1,049.5	3.64	650.0	61.9
Ecuador	182.7	0.63	200.0	109.5[a]
Gabon	188.2	0.65	150.0	79.7[a]
Indonesia	1,469.8	5.10	1,300.0	88.4[a]
Iran	4,500.6	15.62	1,200.0	26.7
Iraq	2,203.4	7.65	1,200.0	54.5
Kuwait	2,249.4	7.80	650.0	28.9
Libya	1,845.7	6.40	750.0	40.6
Nigeria	1,973.5	6.85	1,300.0	65.9[a]
Qatar	482.8	1.68	300.0	62.1
Saudi Arabia	8,459.1	29.35	7,500.0	88.7[a]
UAE	1,688.0	5.86	1,000.0	59.2
Venezuela	2,528.0	8.77	1,500.0	59.3
Neutral Zone	—	—	300.0	—
	28,820.7	100.00	18,000.0	62.5

Note: a. Denotes countries whose new allocations are more than OPEC's average of 62.5 per cent.

Source: *National Concord*, 14 April 1982, p. 4.

expected to cost over ₦80 billion and the monthly import of about ₦1.3 billion were based on a projected crude oil output of 2.3 million barrels a day and at a price of about $35 per barrel. The drop in oil production and a fall in oil price, caused by an excess supply of crudes by both Saudi Arabia and non-OPEC oil producing countries, forced down Nigeria's OPEC production quota to about 650,000 barrels a day in the first week of April, 1982 and Nigeria's foreign reserves reduced to $4.5 billion and then to $3 billion, which was hardly adequate to sustain two months imports. The situation was really critical for Nigeria.

Table 6.1 shows the average production quotas assigned to each member country during the Quito meeting of March, 1982. Nigeria was assigned 1.3 million barrels a day which represented 65.9 per cent of Nigeria's average oil production over the last ten years. The Table also shows the quotas of member countries of OPEC. Table 6.2 on the other hand shows the production levels of member countries by December 1981 and the quantity of output required to balance their current accounts taking into account the prevailing rate of

Table 6.2: Financial Pressures on OPEC Producers and Short-term Output Levels ('000s b/d) (Early 1982)

Country	Financial Reserves $ bn	Output Needed to Balance Current Accounts	Present Output
Saudi Arabia	161.6	6,410	7,900
Libya	33.4	1,070	870
Kuwait	76.2	900	850
UAE	38.6	810	1,400
Qatar	16.1	60	360
Iran	3.0	3,610	950
Iraq	31.8	2,110	950
Nigeria	4.5	2,230	1,800
Algeria	3.8	1,200	700
Gabon	6.7	160	150
Venezuela	7.7	2,400	2,100
Ecuador	0.7	220	200
Indonesia	10.0	1,500	1,600
Total	388.1	22,680	19,830

Source: *National Concord*, 14 April, 1982, p. 4.

imports and also the fall-back reserve positions of OPEC members. It can be seen that Nigeria's deficit production is 672.5 million barrels. If Nigeria is to balance her current account then Nigeria would need an additional 672.5 million barrels a day, but with the present production output level of 750 million barrels a day as of March, 1982 Nigeria's oil production deficit stood at 1.480 million barrels a day. That is to say by April, 1982, an additional 1.480 million barrels a day were required in addition to the 750,000 barrels a day then being produced, if Nigeria was to balance her current account. The calculation was based on the assumption that the OPEC reference price would stand.

The implication was a serious one for Nigeria and nothing short of surgical economic measures were demanded if the economy were to be put back in order. The cash crisis caused by low oil output altered Nigeria's economic variables and parameters. By April, 1982, production had dropped further to 650,000 barrels a day and what was considered a temporary matter was looking more like a permanent condition. When it became obvious that the oil glut and its consequences were no longer temporary matters Nigeria began to recalculate her economic policies and bring about measures to arrest the economic situation from further decline. The Federal Government was forced to take prompt action in order to avert an economic disaster.

The Central Bank of Nigeria took immediate measures of a short-term nature to shore up and lessen the erosion of reserves. In March 1982, all commercial banks in the country were stopped temporarily from processing or issuing letters of credit for imports and requested to stop further processing of applications which would convert Nigerian currency into foreign currency for the payment of incoming imports. These draconian measures shook the foundation of Nigerian business generally, and the immediate reaction was a rise in the price of both imported and Nigerian-made goods.

6. The Economic Stabilisation (Temporary Provisions) Act of 1982 (The Enabling Bill)

On 19 April 1982, the Nigerian National Assembly consisting of both the Senate and the House of Representatives met at an emergency session and empowered the President to take all necessary measures, which he considered proper, to arrest and ameliorate the deplorable situation of the Nigerian economy. In an address to the joint session of the Senate and the House of Representatives the President spoke of the serious nature of the problems of the Nigerian economy and the urgent need for an immediate solution to be found. If certain measures were not taken to stop and reverse the trends with regard to the high rate of importation, foreign exchange disbursement and the expenditures of the federal and state governments, then Nigeria's economy would be doomed. The President painted a gloomy scenario of the Nigerian economic situation. The price of crude oil had fallen as well as daily production which had dropped to 650 barrels per day as against the projected minimum 1.3 million barrels per day, upon which the 1982 budget was projected. The President further stated that the oil companies were reluctant to lift Nigerian crudes and were demanding a further reduction in prices if they were to do so.

As stated earlier the oil companies vigorously denied this accusation. The President entreated the joint session of the House to pass the Enabling Bill to give him the necessary authority to deal summarily with the economic problems of the day. The Enabling Bill was immediately passed by the National Assembly.

7. The Presidential Measures

With the passage of the *Economic Stabilisation (Temporary Provisions)* Act of 1982, the President came out with a sweeping package of measures which astounded the Nigerian business community and consumers, and drew a sigh of relief from international business interests, bilateral and multilateral organisations, who were worried about Nigeria's capacity to stem the economic drift. The measures were aimed at achieving a drastic reduction in imports, especially those items that are not in the priority list, to encourage domestic production, and the correction of the current account of Nigeria's balance of payments position, which had been persistently in deficit.

The presidential measures were far-ranging; they included import measures with fiscal and tariff implications, monetary and banking measures coupled with anti-smuggling controls.

(i) Import Measures

Import measures as contained in the presidential measures can be viewed from three perspectives — import prohibition, import licences and import duties.

(a) Import Prohibition

Before the presidential measures came into force a number of items had already been prohibited. For example, in the 1976/7 financial year champagnes and other aerated drinks as well as imported bottled beers were banned from import. Under the new import measures gaming machines and frozen chicken were completely prohibited from import.

(b) Import Licences

A number of other items were restricted and could only be imported by obtaining fresh import licences for them.

All import licences issued and still valid before the presidential measures were recalled by the Ministry of Commerce and Industries for revalidation and no imports were allowed under such licences unless revalidated. Where goods had already been imported through the use of a licence not revalidated, then such goods were expected to arrive at Nigerian ports within six weeks of the coming into force of the presidential measures. Any imports otherwise made would not have their form M approved by the Central Bank for the payments of such imports.

Items placed under the import licence system are listed below:

(1) Pre-printed papers and forms with or without carbon papers.
(2) All passenger cars.
(3) Plastic pipes.
(4) Yarn of man-made fibre.
(5) Cotton yarn of all types.
(6) Motor tyres for cars with sectional width exceeding 102 mm to 304 mm.
(7) Bolts and nuts including, bolt-ends and screw-studs.
(8) Assembled road and agricultural tractors.
(9) Concentrated malt extracts.
(10) Umbrella handles.
(11) Manufactured articles of wood of all types, including flush doors whether for decorative use or not.
(12) Auto-cycles and cycles.
(13) Cereal flour.
(14) Nails.

(15) Real Madras (George).
(16) Vegetable oil excluding bulk importation.
(17) Processed barite and bentonite.

Apart from the above mentioned items which contributed largely to the naira volume of Nigerian imports, the following items were also placed under import licence: sugar, pick-up delivery vans, wall tiles, baths, water closets, water basins and pans, ceramic sinks and other ceramic products, asbestos cement pipes, furniture fabrics, rice, fishing net, cement, bulk tea and louvre blades; components of the above goods whether assembled or not were restricted except those components allowed under the Approved Users Licence (AUL).

(c) Import Duties

A range of import duties was imposed on items which could be imported under licence. Table 6.3 shows the old import duties and the new duties. Duties on some of the items are based on weight or on a percentage of the value (ad valorem). Whichever is higher becomes the basis of duty for the item.

In addition to Table 6.3, import duties were imposed on parts of locally-assembled passenger cars, lorries, trucks, pick-up vans, delivery vans, road tractors and agricultural tractors imported under CKD (completely knocked down) basis. Other items which attracted various rates were baby carriages, wheelbarrows, motorcycles, autocycles and cycle components. Other goods include batteries, watches, clocks, record players, tape recorders, etc. The rates varied depending on whether those items were completely knocked down and assembled in Nigeria or whether they were partly knocked down and assembled or imported in finished forms.

(d) Excise Duties

Duties on a number of items manufactured in Nigeria such as cigarettes, towels, fabrics of all types, cosmetics, perfumes, paper napkins, serviettes, toilet paper, electric fans, motorcycles, autocycles and bicycles were affected by the new excise rates. Beer breweries and soft drinks industries were excluded from any change in excise duties.

(e) Banking and Foreign Exchange Measures

The major banking measure intended to contain Nigeria's financial crisis was the restructuring of the interest rates of the banking system.

Interest rates were raised by 2 per cent. This naturally led to an increase in the minimum rediscount rate of the Central Bank. It also affected the various deposit rates of the commercial banks

Table 6.3: Import Duties, 1982

Items	Old Duty	New Duty
Stock fish	30% (a.v.)	50% (a.v.)
Bulk tea	10% (a.v.)	50% (concessionary rate of duty abolished)
Rice	10K per kg or 20% (a.v.)	15K per kg or 30% (a.v.)
Cereal flour	15% (a.v.) or ₦10 per tonne	30% (a.v.) or ₦20 per tonne
Beet and cane sugar	5K per kg	10K per kg or 60% (a.v.)
Other sugar	10K per kg or 25% (a.v.)	20K per kg or 60% (a.v.)
Tomatoes	75% or 50K per kg	100% or 70K per kg
Extracts & concentrates of coffee & tea	66% (a.v.)	75% (a.v.)
Cement	—	20% (a.v.)
Baby lotions & creams	200% (a.v.)	33% (a.v.)
Umbrella handles	AUS Abolished	50% (a.v.)
Baby feeding plastic bottles	75% (a.v.)	50% (a.v.)
Tyres for cars	55K per kg	75K per kg
Cigarette paper	5% (a.v.)	10% (a.v.)
Pre-printed papers & forms (with or without carbon)	10% (a.v.)	40% (a.v.)
All forms of yarn	25K per kg or 10% (a.v.)	75K per kg or 30% (a.v.)
Cotton lint	—	5% a.v. (AUS)
Real Madras (George)	₦1 per sq. metre or 100% (a.v.)	₦2 per sq. metre or 200% (a.v.)
Fabrics for imitation leather	1K per sq. metre (AUS)	2K per sq. metre (AUS)
Rubberised textiles	—	50K per sq. metre or 50% a.v. (AUS)
Break linings & disc-pads for motor vehicles	—	60% (a.v.)
Base cloth for lace and embroidery	—	50K per sq. metre or 50% a.v. (AUS)
Iron or steel for pipe and tube manufacture	—	50% a.v. (AUS)
Bolts and nuts and accessories	—	50% (a.v.)
Camera motors and parts	AUS	AUS abolished

Table 6.3 continued

Electric fans	70% (a.v.)	150% (a.v.)
Electric fan components	10% (a.v.)	50% (a.v.)
Electronic equipment (radio, TV, etc)	75% (a.v.)	150% (a.v.)
Electronic components	20% (a.v.)	50% (a.v.)
Electronic parts	10% (a.v.)	50% (a.v.)
Completely knocked down components (CKD)	—	20% a.v. (AUS)
Fabricated structures	30% (a.v.)	40% (a.v.)
Kerosine stoves and parts (CKD)	—	10% a.v. (AUS)
Outboard engine components	10% (a.v.)	50% (a.v.)
Camera and cinemato-graph motors and parts	50% (a.v.)	100% (a.v.)
Generator components	—	10% (AUS)
Electricity supply metres (CKD)	—	50% a.v. (AUS)
Agricultural tractors	—	25% (a.v.)
Pick-up and delivery panel vans	—	100% (a.v.)
Passenger cars	Based on engine capacity and value	Users costs, freight value and engine capacity to determine duty. Whichever is greater, cars exceeding 2,500 cc attract a duty of 500% a.v.
Bicycles and tricycles	—	50% (a.v.)
Motorcycle parts and accessories	10% (a.v.)	20% (a.v.)

Note: a.v. = ad valorem tax. AUS = Approved Users Scheme.

such as Savings rates and Time Deposit rates of various maturities. As a result of the increase of the various rates by 2 per cent the minimum lending rates of Nigerian commercial banks rose to 11 per cent. The new interest rate structure obviously affected the lending rates of specialised institutions such as the Insurance companies, Development and Mortgage banks. The Central Bank was expected to issue new guidelines to the banks and other financial institutions which would take into account the new interest rate structures.

It is however doubtful whether the increase in interest rates will help the financial crisis. It has been empirically established that developing countries are insensitive to a change in the rate of interest. The increase in interest rates may not necessarily reduce borrowing propensities or increase savings propensities dramatically. Savings may only increase as a result of reduced imports which invariably lead to a reduction in consumption.

The most effective of the measures are those which relate to foreign exchange restrictions and compulsory deposit against imports. The major sources of foreign exchange depletion in the Nigerian economy have been established to be basic and business travelling allowances. In 1981 Nigeria spent about ₦3 billion in respect of basic and business travelling allowances. If the prevailing propensity were allowed to continue about ₦5 billion worth of foreign exchange would be spent before the end of the 1982 financial year. The basic and business travelling allowances, as well as allowances to Nigerian pilgrims, were drastically reduced by the presidential measures. Pilgrim entitlements were reduced to ₦800 per adult, and children below 16 years of age no longer qualified for travelling allowances. An ordinary allowance was reduced from ₦800 to ₦500, while a business travelling allowance was reduced to a maximum of ₦2,500. It is estimated that the new measures relating to travel allowances will lead to savings of nearly ₦2 billion in foreign exchange.

Import bills, considered to be the greatest burden on Nigeria's external reserves, were reduced by slowing down the rate of imports and the rate of entering into financial obligations with foreign financiers. In the past, narrow cash margins with the commercial banks were allowed for the purpose of opening letters of credit but the new regulations imposed a higher cash margin. The details of the compulsory deposits under the presidential measures against imports are as follows:

Medicaments — 50% cash deposits based on the total value of imports
Building Materials — 50%
Food Items — 50%, with the exception of rice
Capital goods — 50%
Raw materials — 25%
Spare parts — 25%
Motor vehicles and trucks — 20%.

In the case of motor vehicles and motor cars not only was a full cash deposit equal to the values of those items demanded but an additional deposit of 100 per cent was required. This was to ensure that enough money was made available for customs duties and clearing charges. These categories of goods constitute the biggest drain on Nigerian foreign exchange reserves and therefore attract maximum duties By imposing very high cash deposit margins it was hoped that their importations would be discouraged.

The compulsory advance deposits against imports attracted no interest rates in favour of importers. Deposits for imports under the Usuance Bills were made less rigid. Imports of less than six months maturity under the scheme, that is from the date of shipment of such goods to Nigeria, and bills for calculation and payments on account of less than six months duration from the date of shipment of such goods to Nigeria require advance deposits on or before the arrival of the vessels carrying such goods to any Nigerian port. Payments not made accordingly will lead to the importer forfeiting foreign exchange allocation for the payment of such imports. All deposits against imports were to be lodged with the Central Bank. The registration of Form M was also made more difficult as various processes approved by the Central Bank have to be followed.

(f) Anti-smuggling Measures

To back up the import restriction measures, provisions for the strengthening of the anti-smuggling task forces and the X-Squad were made. Officers of such task forces, the X-Squad and other informants were to be adequately remunerated. More container depots and X-ray equipment for the identification of the contents of containers were to be acquired. The unpopular customs raids on markets and warehouses were to continue. Seaports, Nigerian coastal waters and airports were to be more thoroughly guarded than before. In order to enhance the efficiency of anti-smuggling officers and their informants a training centre was to be established. Stiff penalties awaited clearing and forwarding agents who colluded with smugglers as well as corrupt customs officials who make deals with businessmen. Clearing and forwarding agents were to be screened in order to prune their number. Those found guilty of abetting smuggling would be closed down.

The presidential measures are probably the stiffest measures that have ever been imposed on the Nigerian economy. It is speculated that if the measures are adequately enforced the Nigerian economy may recover. The external reserve level may rise up to ₦10 billion before the end of 1982. Political observers believe that the presidential measures may not only put Nigeria back onto the proper economic course but will also help the governing party, the National Party of Nigeria, at the general election which is expected to begin in June or July, 1983. It would be in the interest of the governing party which formed the Nigerian Federal Government if a clean balance sheet were presented to the electorate. Opposing political parties have accused the governing party of 'squandermania' and misplacement of priorities. If by the end of 1982 the economy picks up as expected, the rigid but necessary economy measures will be relaxed as the election months draw near.

References and Additional Reading

Annual Statistical Bulletin, OPEC Information Department, Organization of Petroleum Exporting Countries, Vienna

'Black Market and The Nigerian Economy', in the *Business Times*, Lagos, 10 May 1982

CBN, *Annual Report and Statement of Accounts*, Lagos, (Annually)

'CBN Circulars Create Uneasiness for Businessmen', in the *Business Times*, Lagos, 29 March 1982

CBN, *Economic and Financial Review*, Lagos, (Biannually)

'CBN Measures May Jeopardise Economy', in the *Financial Punch*, 5 April 1982

'Closure of Private Jetties Generates Controversy', in the *Business Times*, Lagos, 26 April 1982

'Commercial Banks Yet to Comply with CBN's Directive', in the *Nigerian Statesman*, Owerri, 31 March 1982

'Economic Stabilization, 1982 Temporary Provisions Act', in the Business Times, Lagos, 17 May 1982

'Effective Management of External Debt', in the *Business Times*, Lagos, 10 May 1982

El Mallakh, Ragaei (ed.), 'Energy Options and Conservation', in Proceedings of the Fourth International Energy Conference, International Research Center for Energy and Economic Development, University of Colorado, Boulder, Colorado, Forthcoming, 1978

'Enabling Bill Sails Through', in the *Daily Times*, Lagos, 21 April 1982

'Foreign Reserve Falls Sharply', in the *Businss Times*, Lagos, 26 April 1982

'How to Break our Dependence on Oil', in the *Daily Times*, 31 March 1982

'Industrialists React to CBN Order', in the *Business Times*, Lagos, 29 March 1982

'More Details on Import Restrictions', in the *Nigerian Statesman*, Owerri, 23 April 1982

'Nigeria Advised to Re-order Priorities', in the *Business Times*, Lagos, 19 April 1982

'Nigeria and the Oil Market', in the *National Concord*, Lagos, 14 April 1982

'Nigeria to Consume 4.6m Tonnes of Petrol in 1983', in the *Business Times*, Lagos, 12 April 1982

'Non-cooperation Between Central Bank and Ministry of Finance', in the *National Concord*, Lagos, 31 March 1982

'Oil Companies Deny Allegation', in the *Business Times*, Lagos, 19 April 1982

'Oil Experts Lack Foresight', in the *Punch*, Lagos, 26 April 1982

'Oil Production Drop: Is it a Conspiracy?', in the *Business Times*, Lagos, 19 April 1982

'Oil Production Increases', in the *Business Times*, Lagos, 10 May 1982

'Oil Production Picks Up', in the *Nigerian Standard*, Jos, 22 May 1982

Onoh, J.K., *Central Bank of Nigeria: Monetary Policies and the Economy*, Fourth Dimension Publishing Co., Enugu, 1982

Onoh, J.K., *Money and Banking in Africa*, Longman, London/Lagos/New York, 1982

Park, S., *The World Oil Economy in the 1970s*, West-View Press, Boulder, Colorado, 1976

'Payment For Imports Under Letters of Credit', in the *Business Times*, Lagos, 29 March 1982

'President's Austerity Broadcast', in the *Nigerian Statesman*, 22 April 1982

'Private Jetties and the Economy', in the *Daily Times*, Lagos, 26 April 1982

'Shehu Takes Drastic Measures', in *Punch*, Lagos, 21 April 1982

'Stockfish, Rice, Cement, Pick-up and Panel Vans Duties Go Up', in the *Nigerian Statesman*, Owerri, 22 April 1982

'The Central Bank Directive', in the *Financial Punch*, Lagos, 29 March 1982

'The Crisis: Consensus against Devaluation', in the *Financial Punch*, 5 April 1981

'The Economy and Nigerians', in the *Daily Times*, Lagos, 24 April 1982

'The Faltering Boom', in the *Financial Punch*, Lagos, 29 March 1982

'The Ups and Downs of Nigeria's Oil Fortune', in the *Daily Times*, Lagos, 29 March 1982

'Time For Hard Decision', in the *Business Times*, Lagos, 29 March 1982

'Up-turn Expected in June', in the *Business Times*, Lagos, 12 April 1982

'Why Gold has Joined Oil in Eclipse', in the *Nigerian Statesman*, Owerri, 26 April 1982

'World Bank Taken to Task', in the *Daily Times*, Lagos, 19 April 1982

7 OIL IN NIGERIAN POLITICS

Nigeria is the most populous country in Africa. It has more than 300 ethnic groups speaking different languages. The diversity in language and culture has a very strong bearing on the Nigerian political scene. Ethnic considerations have also brought their weight to bear on the oil revenue allocation formula which constituted one of the toughest political issues in the annals of Nigeria's history as a political entity. In spite of the avowed determination of the country's leaders to forge a united country, the social and ethnic diversities notwithstanding, a detached observer of the Nigerian political scene will notice that political parties still fall very strongly along tribal lines with each party manoeuvring to ensure that the area or areas it controls obtains a larger share of what in Nigerian political parlance is called the national cake.

Since the 1960s, when oil was discovered in large quantities in Nigeria, the sharing of oil revenue among the regions (states) has been a very knotty problem. Oil revenue and the sharing formula have become important elements in Nigerian politics. Apart from the oil wells of the Imo State of Nigeria, which lies in Igbo land (the Igbos constitute one of Nigeria's major tribal groups beside the Yoruba group of the West and the Fulani/Hausa groups of the North), most of the oil discoveries have been mainly in the minority tribe areas of Bendel State, Rivers State and Cross River State of Nigeria. These minority states constitute Nigeria's political buffer states. They are determined to secure a larger portion of the oil revenue for themselves on the basis of the derivation principle. Because of the riotous number of ethnic groups within these states and because of their minority populations they have been unable to wield a very strong influence in Nigerian politics or secure a large portion of the oil revenue. Appreciating their weak positions they have tended to align with one or two of the political parties which have the backing of the major tribal groups in order to achieve what they believe to be their rights to a greater share of Nigeria's oil revenue. The minorities are striving to form themselves into a force that can be reckoned with in tilting the balance of Nigeria's domestic politics. Oil revenue has become a very important element in Nigeria's political scenario. In the 1960s it contributed largely to the Nigeria/Biafra war. In the late

1970s it was applied internationally to gain for Nigeria a political leverage in world affairs. Before discussing the details of the significance of oil and oil revenue sharing in Nigerian politics it is desirable to examine the genesis of revenue sharing in Nigeria.

1. Genesis of Revenue Sharing in Nigeria

Revenue sharing in Nigeria has similar objectives to achieve as those clearly stated in Nigeria's Second National Development Plan (1970/4). The objectives of the Plan are as follows:—

(i)   A united, strong and self-reliant nation;
(ii) A great and dynamic economy;
(iii) A just and egalitarian society;
(iv) A land of pride and full opportunities for all societies, and
(v)   A free and democratic society.

Since Nigeria became a political entity eight committees charged with the functions of designing a suitable revenue sharing formula for Nigeria have so far been set up. The frequency with which these committees are set up is evidence that the recommendations of preceding committees were not universally acceptable to all political shades in the country.

The revenue sharing formula has been made more complex by the changes in the political structure of the country. In 1914 Northern and Southern Nigeria were amalgamated by Lord Lugard to form the political entity called Nigeria. A number of constitutional changes in the 1940s led to political restructuring of the country. Three regions emerged from the constitutional changes. North, West and Eastern Regions and the Lagos Colony, which originally formed a part of the Western regions, were created. In the early 1960s another region was created from the Western region and called the Midwest region. Midwest was later renamed the Bendel State of Nigeria. In May, 1967, during the civilian upheaval, the Federal Military Government in power created twelve states. The Northern, Western and the Eastern Regions were split into smaller political units to accommodate the feelings and demands of the minorities of Nigeria who wanted states of their own instead of being grouped together with the majority tribes of the three main regions.

In 1976 another military government which came to power created 19 states in the federation thereby breaking up Nigeria into much smaller units. Each time new states were created the political strength of the mother regions or states was reduced. As the powerful regions became weakened with the creation of more states the power of the central government invariably increased. The changes from a civilian government to a military government and from one military government to another military government brought with them changes in revenue allocations which were also not widely accepted. With the creation of more and more states the voices of the minority tribes became more vocal in Nigerian politics. They began to insist on a revenue sharing formula which would be more favourable to them, because most of the oil discoveries were made in the minority tribal areas of Bendel, Cross River and Rivers States and in the offshore locations bordering these coastal states.

2. Revenue Sharing Formula in the 1940s and 1950s

These were the colonial periods when revenue sharing was not so politicised as it is today. Revenue sharing in the colonial era did take a factor into consideration: the autonomy of the regions. The autonomy of the regions has, since the creation of states, been equated to the autonomy of states.

Before 1953 the central government had full power over revenue. It only allocated revenue to the regions on the basis of derivation, after the central government had been able to meet its own obligations. But as Nigeria progressed towards self-government a new revenue policy became very pertinent in view of the creation of regions which were expected to be politically powerful after self-government. If the regions were to exercise their political powers effectively they would have to enjoy a measure of financial independence. In 1953 a committee headed by Sir Louis Chick was set up. The committee was required to design a revenue sharing formula between the regions and the centre which would provide both the centre and the regions a good measure of fiscal autonomy, and which would take into consideration the principle of derivation. Chick's report recommended a revenue sharing formula based strongly on the principle of derivation. For example, mining rents and royalties imposed and collected by the

Federal Government were channelled to the treasuries of the regions from which those minerals were extracted. Import duties on motor spirit and tobacco were returned 100 per cent and 50 per cent respectively to the regions according to consumption. 15 per cent of other goods other than motor spirit and tobacco were shared among the regions as follows: North 15 per cent, West 20 per cent and East 14.5 per cent. Personal income taxes were returned to the regions in which the tax payer resided, even though such taxes were collected by the Federal Government. Mining rents and royalties were returned to regions of origin but company taxes were retained by the centre.

In 1958, another revenue sharing committee was set up headed by Sir Jeremy Raisman which did not abolish the principle of derivation but added other criteria. Raisman allocated a percentage of mining, rents and royalties to the Federal Government. Still the regions had all the advantages. The new recommendations of Raisman did not depress the fiscal autonomy of the regions *vis à vis* the Federal Government. In addition to the derivation principle, Raisman recommended the following criteria for the purpose of revenue allocation:

(a) relative populations of the regions;
(b) the responsibilities of each regional government;
(c) continuity of the regional public services;
(d) balanced development of the regions;
(e) balancing of the revenue short-falls of the regions;
(f) the retention of export duties on produce, hides and skins by the regions of origin;
(g) the sharing of import duties on motor spirit and diesel oil on the basis of consumption;
(h) the splitting of mining rents and royalties between the regions and the federal government as follows:
    (i) 50% to the regions of origin (derivation principle)
    (ii) 20% to the Federal Government and
    (iii) 30% to be channelled to the distributable Pools Account (DPA) to be shared between the regions as follows:
    North   —   40%
    East   —   31%
    West   —   24%

3. Revenue Allocation in the 1960s

Under the 1963 Constitution the regions retained more revenue and were relatively wealthier than the Federal Government. The financial autonomy and wealth of the regions gained them a political power that tended to weaken the Federal Government. The financial position of the regions was later to be trimmed by the military governments which came to power in the 1960s and 1970s, which emphasised a strong centre and weak regions (states) as opposed to the concept of strong regions and a weak centre of the 1950s and early 1960s.

The Nigerian Constitution of 1963, which was drawn up shortly after Nigeria's independence, reviewed revenue sources and allocations. The Federal Government was given tax jurisdiction over import duties, export duties, excise duties, mining rents and royalties, petroleum profit tax and company tax, which the Federal Government had always retained. Personal income tax and capital gains tax originally under state jurisdiction were later to be transferred to the Federal Government in 1975 while the administration and retention of the revenue remained with the states.

Under the 1963 Constitution, import duties from tobacco, motor spirit and fuel were allocated wholly to the regions while beverages (beer, wine and spirits) were allocated *in toto* to the Federal Government. Duties from other imports were shared in the ratio of 65:35 between the federal and regional governments. Exports duties on all produce, hides and skins were allocated entirely to the regions of origin. Excise duties went to the Federal Government with the exception of tobacco and motor fuels which were allocated to the regions. Mining rents and royalties were shared as follows:

15% to the Federal Government;
50% to the regions of origin (principle of derivation); and
35% of mining, royalties and rents were allocated to the Distributable Pools Account for distribution to the regions according to the Raisman formula stated above.

Until 1967 the regional governments retained over 70 per cent of federally collected revenue. This was in addition to the tax jurisdiction allowed them by the 1963 Nigerian Constitution. The regions were allowed by the 1963 Constitution to collect sales and purchase taxes, produce and other duties, entertainment tax, cattle tax, football pools tax, betting taxes, motor vehicle and drivers' licence fees. When another Federal Military Government came to power in 1976 it discovered the apparent weak financial position of the centre and decided to introduce measures to reduce drastically the financial autonomies of the states it had carved out from the regions in May, 1967. Through decrees the states were left with less than 25 per cent of federally collected revenue as against the 70 per cent enjoyed by the regions before the military government came to power in January, 1966.

When they were only four regions the Distributable Pools Account was allocated as follows:

North	—	42%
East	—	30%
West	—	20%
Midwest	—	8%

When the twelve States were created in 1967 the allocations became as follows for the States in the Southern region:

East Central State	—	17.5%
South East	—	7.5%
Rivers State	—	5%
Western State	—	18%
Lagos State	—	2%

In the case of the seven Northern States which made up the former Northern region the 42 per cent of the DPA allocated to the former Northern region was shared equally among the states. The equal sharing formula used by the Northern states was disputed by the more populous states of the Northern region.

4. Oil Politics in the Nigeria/Biafra War

In January, 1966 the military government came to power as the nation grew tired with the incompetent and corrupt federal and regional governments. The takeover of the central government by the military was given a tribal interpretation. The Northern region in particular, peopled by the Hausas and Fulanis, was of the opinion that the military coup was masterminded by the Igbos who inhabited mainly the Eastern region of Nigeria. They claimed that during the military coup mostly Northern and Western politicians were killed but the popular Igbo politicians escaped unhurt. Emotion was stirred up in the North. Many Igbos who lived in the Northern region were systematically massacred or maimed. Others escaped to the Eastern region. Those who escaped to the East returned to the Northern region as the situation calmed down, following an appeal by the Northern Emirs and the then Governor of the Eastern Region, Col. Odumegwu Ojukwu.

In July, 1966 there was a counter military coup which this time was masterminded by the officers and men from the Northern region. More massacres of the Igbos took place in the Northern region. The then governor of the Eastern region, who was an Igbo, Col. Odumegwu Ojukwu (later Gen. Ojukwu during the Biafra regime) ordered Igbos and the minority tribes of the Eastern region living in the North to return to the East as their security could no longer be guaranteed. In view of the grave situation Col. Ojukwu on the mandate of the people of the Eastern region demanded a loose federation (confederation). Several discussions took place in Aburi, Ghana, under the Chairmanship of General Ankrah, the then Head of the Ghana military government. A confederation was agreed between Lt. Col. Gowon, the then Nigerian Head of State (later Gen. Gowon) and Lt. Col. Odumegwu Ojukwu the Governor of the Eastern region. Following advice he received on his return from Ghana, Lt. Col. Gowon refused to abide by the Aburi agreement, which recommended a loose federation if Nigeria should survive as a unit. Gowon's political advisers analysed for him the economic implications of the proposed confederation. It would mean a large measure of autonomy for the regions in which the Eastern region stood to benefit largely from the oil revenue derived from the large oil reserves of the Eastern region to the disadvantage of the Federal Government and the other regions. Col. Ojukwu insisted on the Aburi agreement. Col. Gowon on the other hand declared the Aburi agreement a non-starter. After the pressure from the people of the then Eastern Region, Col. Ojukwu declared the Republic of Biafra on 30 May 1967.

Oil became an important factor during the war. Some analysts argued that Ojukwu intended to strangulate the economies of the rest of Nigeria. Others were of the opinion that Ojukwu declared the Republic of Biafra in order to provide for the people of Biafra the security and the sense of belonging denied to them in Nigeria. Nigeria on the other hand argued that it was not because of oil that it was declaring war on Biafra but because Nigeria must be kept united in the interests of Africa. Some political pundits began to forecast that a disintegration of Nigeria would lead to a disintegration of the other countries of Africa as most African nations consisted of an amalgam of incoherent tribes forged together as nations through the might of colonial governments. Both sides (Nigeria and Biafra) began to use the oil factor as an instrument of propaganda to their best advantages within and outside Nigeria. Ojukwu insisted that the oil companies operating in the Eastern region should pay rents and royalties, which had been under the jurisdiction of the Federal Government following the 1963 Constitution, into the coffers of the Government of Biafra. The Nigerian Federal Goverment on the other hand threatened that any oil company that paid rents or royalties to the Biafran government would have its licence revoked and assets confiscated. The oil companies were thrown to the centre of the chessboard of Nigerian power politics. Throughout the greater part of the war, especially in the early months, it was well known that oil companies paid rents and royalties to both sides in order to ensure their survival, whichever side won.

The French oil company Safrap, now called Elf, was accused by the Nigerian Federal Government of leaning more to Biafra and of allegedly securing political and military support for Biafra. Safrap being a company of French origin became all the more suspect because of sympathy shown by French people and the top hierarchy of the Government of France towards Biafra, and because of the formal recognition of Biafra by three French-speaking countries: Ivory Coast, Gabon and the former French-speaking West Indian colony, the Republic of Haiti. Rife also was a rumour of overflowing sympathy among the rank and file of the ruling government of Tunisia which was also a former French colony. Shell BP, a company with British interests and oldest of the foreign oil companies, and which operated mainly in the Eastern region, began to circulate the rumour that Safrap was aiding Biafra politically and militarily and that the Biafran Government had promised to revoke Shell's licence after the war and to hand over the licence to Safrap, the French Oil Company.

Wherever foreign oil companies operate, it is said the hearts of their governments lie there also. While Shell BP canvassed British support for Nigeria and the immediate destruction of Biafra in order to retain its oil interests in the Region, Safrap canvassed for French diplomatic and military support for Biafra. Two Western powers, Britain and France, experienced a conflict of interests in Nigeria. Eventually Nigeria won the war and Shell BP retained its influence. The oil exploration and exploitation licences of Safrap were not revoked by Nigeria for fear of offending the French Government, but Nigeria went on to acquire 35 per cent of the equity interests of Safrap, now called Elf. Nigeria was cautious in her approach to Safrap knowing full well that Nigeria's application to the European Economic Community for admission as an associate member had not yet been conclusively decided, and the French had a veto power. Any serious action against Safrap might have evoked a French veto when Nigeria's application for associate membership of the EEC came under formal discussion. Throughout the war Nigeria avoided any open propaganda against the French government, fearing the French veto.

On the domestic front oil also became an important issue. Most of the oil discovered in the Eastern region was found mainly in the non-Igbo speaking areas of the region. Both the Federal Government and the Biafran Government jockeyed for the support of the minority parties in the Eastern region. As the rumour of Biafra's secession gathered momentum Gowon pre-empted the declaration by creating states in Nigeria, whereby the Eastern region which was shortly to be declared Biafra was split into three states. One state for the majority Igbos and two states for the minorities region in whose areas most of the oil wells were located. The war propaganda machinery was let loose. Radio Nigeria continuously reminded the minorities that through the creation of the new states the minorities had been given the autonomy they had sought for years. Economically the minorities would benefit from revenue arising from rents and royalties which would be paid directly to their states' treasuries, instead of the Biafran treasury at Enugu. The minorities were further told that under Biafra the more dominant Igbos would utilise oil revenues to develop the Igbo areas to the neglect and detriment of the minority areas, but with the creation of the new states, the minorities remaining under the aegis of Nigeria would control their own destinies.

Radio Biafra countered the propaganda by reminding the minorities that they were Christians and that the predominantly Moslem region of the North which under Gowon controlled the Federal Government had never had their interests at heart. The minorities were to be massacred in the North just as were the Igbos, and no distinction was to be made between Igbos and the minorities during the pogrom. If Biafra lost the war the oil revenue from the minority areas would be used to develop the Northern region without recourse to the welfare of the minorities. By simple arithmetic if the oil revenue were shared among the three provinces which constituted Biafra, each province would gain more than if it were shared among the twelve states created by Gowon. The minorities became divided in their loyalties: propaganda and counter propaganda on the relative advantages of being under Nigeria or under Biafra was broadcast daily. Consequently the minorities who before the beginning of the war had been on the side of Biafra began to waiver. As the war progressed to the advantage of Nigeria a greater proportion of the minorities began to desert Biafra for Nigeria in the hope that if Nigeria won the greater bulk of the oil revenue would accrue to them for the infrastructural, social and economic development of their minority areas. How the hope was realised or shattered will be discussed in the following section.

5. Revenue Allocation Since the 1970s

Shortly before the end of the civil war, another revenue allocation review Committee was set up in 1969 and headed by Mr I.O. Dina. The recommendations of the Committee yielded Decree No. 13 of 1970 which enhanced the revenue powers of the Federal Government *vis à vis* the states. Excise duties and sales of tobacco and petroleum products which were shared between the regions and later between the states on the basis of consumption were now to be shared to the extent of 50 per cent to the Federal Government and 50 per cent to to DPA for reallocation to the states. Export duties of produce, hides and skins, which formerly were allocated to the regions and later to the states of origin on the basis of derivation were, under decree No. 13 of 1970, shared between the states of origin and the DPA in the ratio of 3 to 2.

Mining rents and royalties which under the former allocation formula allowed the states 50 per cent on the basis of derivation, 15 per cent to the Federal Government and 35 per cent to the DPA were, according to Decree No. 13 of 1970, to be shared as follows:

State of Derivation	—	45%
Federal Government	—	5%
DPA	—	50%

Import duties on motor spirit and fuel which were allocated to the states on the principle of relative consumption were shared equally between the Federal Government and State Governments on a 50/50 basis. Finally, the DPA sharing formula was drastically altered to take only two principles into consideration — the equality and population of the states, whereby 50 per cent of the DPA was shared among the states equally and 50 per cent on the basis of population. This formula shocked the minority states of Bendel, Rivers and Cross River where most of the oil fields are located. Contrary to the wartime promise by the Federal Government that the principle of derivation would continue to form an important element for the revenue allocation formula, that principle was completely eliminated for the first time by the Dina Report. The two revenue sharing principles of equality of states and the strength of population did not give the minority states any of the advantages they expected in a country where oil revenue contributed over 85 per cent of the national income. The populations of the minority states of Bendel, Rivers and Cross River were relatively small when compared to those of the Western states, Kano State, Kaduna State and the East Central State peopled by the Igbos. The minorities felt cheated by the Dina formula. The most populous states of Nigeria continued to take away the greater portion of the oil revenue on the one hand, while the Federal Government's own share of the oil revenue continued to increase to the disadvantage of the oil producing minority areas.

In 1971 an addition to the revenue formula was introduced by the *Offshore Oil Revenue Decree No. 9* of 1971. Under the Decree the Federal Governnment received all offshore oil revenue; the offshore wells were located in the coastal waters adjoining the oil producing minority states. The three oil minority states were again angered by the new measure. They insisted that their states should participate in the sharing of the offshore oil revenue as the offshore explorations affected fishery, the main economic activity of the riverine areas.

The revenue problems of the states were compounded by the abolition of the Marketing Boards which had provided major sources of revenue to the regions and the establishment of Commodity Boards to replace the Marketing Boards. The Commodity Boards were placed under the Federal Government. The introduction of uniform tax in the 1975/6 financial year through the *Uniform Tax Decree No. 7* of 1975 further aggravated the revenue problems of the states (oil and non-oil). The uniform tax rate did not allow the states to vary tax rates. The introduction of uniform retail prices for petroleum products also harmed the ability of the states to levy sales tax on petroleum products. Such sales taxes in the past were a major source of revenue to the states.

Because of the protests of the oil producing states — Bendel, Rivers, Cross River and Imo State — amendments were made to the existing revenue sharing formula which only took into consideration the principles of population and equality of States. Decree No. 6 of 1975 amended the allocations as follows:

(a) Excise duties were to be shared on 50/50 basis between the Federal and State Governments where such duties were collected.

(b) Twenty per cent of onshore receipts (mining rents and royalties) were to be channelled to the region of origin following the principle of derivation, while the remaining 80 per cent of onshore receipts were to be channelled to the Distributable Pools Account (DPA). All offshore receipts were to be channelled *in toto* to the DPA.

No revenue allocation formula, it seems, can satisfy the yearning of all Nigerians. With the preparations towards a return to a civilian government in 1979 a Constitution Drafting Committee was set up. Revenue sharing was in the terms of reference. The Constitution Drafting Committee set up a technical committee to advise it on what was a thorny issue. The Committee headed by Professor O. Aboyade was to examine the problems of revenue allocation, especially with respect to the three tiers of governments (i.e. Federal, State and Local Governments) which were envisaged under the new constitution. Aboyade's Committee Report was again a disappointment to the minority oil producing states as well as to Imo State. (Imo State is peopled by Igbos. The state is not regarded as a minority state.) The Committee's Report abolished entirely the principle of derivation upon which the hopes of the oil producing states had been centred. Aboyade's Committee report recommended the consolidation of all federally collected revenue into one account and to be shared as follows:

Federal Government	57%
States' Government	30%
Local Government	10%
Special Grants accounts	
(to be administered by the	
Federal Government)	3%
Total	100%

States Joint Account was to be shared among the States taking the following weights into consideration:

(i)	Equality of State	0.25%
(ii)	National Minimum Standard	0.22%
(iii)	Absorptive Capacity	0.20%
(iv)	Independent Revenue	0.18%
(v)	Fiscal Efficiency	0.15%
		1.00%

Aboyade's criteria for computing these weights were found very difficult to apply. In addition to the revenue of 10 per cent to be allocated to the local governments from the centre the state governments were expected to allocate a further 10 per cent of each state's portion of the States Joint Account to their local governments. In accepting the report the Federal Government merged the 3 per cent special grant meant for the rehabilitation of polluted oil producing areas, national emergencies, disasters and environmental problems with the 50 per cent allocated to the Federal Government and designated it as contingency funds, which the Federal Government would manage.

The Aboyade committee report was found too cumbersome in

application. Consequently when the civilian administration took over the reins of government on 1 October 1979, the pressure for a new revenue formula was very great. President Shehu Shagari had to set up the Okigbo Commission on Revenue Allocation to re-examine the issue. Okigbo's commission travelled around the states and received hundreds of memoranda with ideas on how best to share the federally collected revenue. The oil producing states laid emphasis on derivation, the populous states emphasised population while large states such as Gongola, Yola and Sokoto emphasised land area. The suggestion of land area created a new dimension in the history of revenue allocation in Nigeria. All the states wanted the federal portion of the revenue to be drastically reduced to the advantage of the states. The representatives of the Federal Government on the other hand claimed that in view of the enormous responsibilities imposed on the Federal Government by the new constitution, the Federal Government should be given 80 per cent of all federally collected revenue.

After considering all opinions, the Okigbo Commission arrived at the following revenue sharing formula:

Federal Government	—	53%
State Governments	—	30%
Local Governments	—	10%
Special Funds	—	7%

The special funds were to be applied as follows:

Federal Capital Territory	—	2.5%
Problems of Mineral Producing Areas	—	2%
Natural Disasters and Environmental Problems	—	1%
Revenue Equalisation Fund	—	1.5%

Okigbo's commission also upheld the claim of the oil producing states that they should benefit from both the onshore and offshore revenue. However the oil producing states suffered another setback as the Okigbo Commission failed to uphold the principle of derivation because the principle was considered more of a political principle rather than a legal right.

For the state government's share of the federally collected revenue the following principles were to be applied:

(i) Minimum responsibilities of government;
(ii) Development oriented factors (e.g. primary School enrolment) (Direct and Inverse);
(iii) Internal revenue effort of states.

The following weights were attached to the above principles:

(i) Minimum responsibility of government	—	40%
(ii) Population	—	40%
(iii) Social development factor (primary school)		
Direct enrolment 15 per cent, whereby	—	11.25%
Inverse enrolment	—	3.75%
(iv) Internal revenue effort	—	5%
Total	—	100%

Okigbo's commission report was accepted with some amendments by the Federal Government. For example the principle of derivation was adopted but the participation of states in offshore derived revenue by Okigbo was not accepted in principle. The National Assembly recommended the following sharing formula for the three tiers of government:

(i) Federal Government	—	55%
(ii) State Governments	—	30%
(iii) Local Governments	—	8%
(iv) Special Fund	—	7%

The special fund was applied as follows:

Mineral producing areas	—	3.5%
Development of Mineral Producing Areas	—	1.5%
Federal capital territory and ecological problems	—	1.0%

A Joint Committee of the National Assembly approved the Federal Government white papers but unfortunately these were not referred back to the National Assembly for endorsement before the Presidential assent. The approval was challenged in the High Court and annulled for reasons of unconstitutionality in the procedure.

Consequently another revenue bill went to the house which was properly passed as follows:

Federal Government	—	55%
State Government	—	35%
Local Government	—	10%

The 35 per cent allocation to the State Governments was broken down as follows:

Direct to the States	—	30%
Derivation	—	2%
Development of Mineral Producing Areas	—	1.5%
Ecological Problems	—	1.5%

The Federal Government's share of revenue was drastically reduced from its pre-1975 figure of about 80 per cent to 55 per cent. Local governments were given added responsibilities including health and education which had hitherto rested squarely with the state governments. The weights evolved by Okigbo for sharing the 30 per cent of the federally collected revenue among the states still applied. It does not appear that the present formula is still satisfactory to all even though it has been formally approved on democratic principles. Revenue sharing is, however, a continuous exercise.

There is no doubt that oil revenue has been a prominent factor in Nigerian politics from the 1960s to the 1980s. Nigeria is in sixth position among the world's ten largest producers of oil. Nigeria has become very significant in terms of the world economy and also in terms of world politics. Having witnessed the political impacts of the Arab oil embargo on the Western nations during the Arab/Israeli war, Nigeria has realised that oil really can be used as an effective instrument of diplomacy and of reversing the role of political arm-twisting, which until the 1970s had been the monopoly of Western countries, and which was applied to aid-hungry Third World countries. In 1978, history was made when President Carter landed with his entourage to pay a state visit to Nigeria. It was likened to the landing of UFO's on earth from remote galaxies. Whatever compels a President of the United States to step out from the United States and curry the friendship of a Third World country must be very pressing indeed. The strained relationship with Iran resulting from the overthhrow of the late Shah of Iran, his replacement by the Iranian Revolutionary government of Ayatollah Khomeini, and the granting of political asylum to the Shah by the United States government, led to the cutting off of Iranian oil supplies to the United States. Having lost a major source of oil supply, President Carter visited Nigeria to request the stepping up of Nigeria's oil production in order that the US might make up the difference created by the Iranian oil embargo. Nigeria is the second largest supplier of oil to the United States, and contributes almost 20 per cent of the United States' total oil imports.

Nigeria was eager to increase her oil supplies to the United States in an effort to influence US policy in Africa. Nigerian political interests included the United States' role in Angola, the nonchalant US attitude towards Namibian independence, the lack of effective US pressure on Britain to influence the development of majority rule in Zimbabwe and the United States' huge investments in South Africa which continued to increase inspite of an outcry from the African countries against apartheid, and also the consistent US veto against the application of an economic embargo or military pressure on South Africa. The then President of the United States, Mr Jimmy Carter had all the reasons to visit Nigeria and to gain favour with the Nigerian military government in view of the unpredictability of the policies of military governments. Andrew Young, the former black American Ambassador to the UN played a very significant role in cementing economic and political relationships between Nigeria and the United States during the Carter era. But for America's own interests, Nigeria could not have become overnight such an important region for America's new shuttle diplomacy.

In 1979 Nigeria's oil was again used to Africa's advantage and this time against the Iron Lady, Mrs Thatcher, whose policies towards Zimbabwe (in the eyes of African countries) tended towards the continuation of the white minority government in Zimbabwe. During the Commonwealth Leaders Conference held in Lusaka in the autumn of 1979, Nigeria struck a political and economic blow to the astonishment of the entire world. Information reaching the Nigerian Government indicated that Mrs

Thatcher intended to deliver a speech which in effect would mean *de facto* recognition of the minority government in Zimbabwe. Nigeria had to act very fast to pre-empt the British by announcing in Lusaka the immediate nationalisation of British Petroleum assets in Nigeria amounting to several millions of naira. BP is the largest single British investment in Nigeria. Nigeria threatened further nationalisation of all British assets in Nigeria worth over one billion naira if the UK did not change her policy on Zimbabwe. The British delegation was shocked and hurriedly prepared a new speech for Mrs Thatcher directed towards finding a quick solution towards majority rule in Zimbabwe. Nigeria's action was praised by African countries and by other Third World countries. A timetable was quickly set up by the British government for Zimbabwe's independence. The UK had to act quickly as the Nigerian government had not clarified its position as to whether nationalisation of BP assets would be compensated or not. To an extent, it can be said that Zimbabwe owes its independence to Nigeria. Nigeria had used her oil to consolidate her position as a pacesetter in African politics, a position which had eluded her for two decades.

References and Additional Reading

'Nigeria and Oil Diplomacy', in the *Daily Times*, Lagos, 2 Oct. 1981

'Oil Companies Strapped', in the *Financial Punch*, Lagos, 29 March 1982

Onoh, J.K. (Ed.) *The Foundations of Nigeria's Financial Infrastructure*, Croom Helm, London, 1981

'Revenue Allocation, Management of Economy', in the *Business Times*, Lagos, 3 May 1982

'Revenue Allocation and Management of the Economy', in the *Business Times*, 10 May 1982

8 OIL IN INTERNATIONAL ECONOMIC AND POWER POLITICS IN THE 1970s AND 1980s

Since the depression of the early 1930s never has the world economy been so threatened as in the 1970s and 1980s. Inflation reached an unprecedented level for most advanced countries and for all developing countries, which are import-dependent. The cost of production rose dramatically and recession, accompanied by a high level of unemployment and high interest rates, characterised the economies of the advanced countries. The industrialised countries were panic-stricken. Economic ills which affect industrialised countries obviously spread to developing countries in multiple ways.

The single factor which has contributed most to the world economic gloom of the 1970s and 1980s is oil. The dramatic downswing of the world economy was caused by rising oil prices. The rise in oil prices was caused by a number of factors. The world's major consuming countries falsely believed that the era of cheap oil would continue. They lacked foresight and made no effort to find substitute sources of energy. The demand for oil by the industrialised countries increased faster than it took to discover new oil wells. The awareness of oil producing countries of the increasing importance of oil in the world economy and international politics and diplomacy helped to push oil prices up, and political constellations in the Middle East accelerated the dramatic change in the world oil scenario.

1. The OPEC Factor

The Organisation of Petroleum-Exporting Countries established in 1960 is a union of the major oil producing countries. Its main objectives include the full participation of its members in all spheres of the oil industry such as exploitation, exploration and the fixing of prices of crudes.

For decades oil multinationals of American, British, French and Anglo-Dutch origins were the masters of the world oil industry. They invested their funds, determined the oil production level and fixed the prices of oil and oil products. They also determined the regions where oil production was to be stepped up or down, with the objective of achieving maximum profits for their companies. Before the 1960s oil was in abundance. Supply of oil exceeded demand. Oil became one of the cheapest energy sources for the industrialised world. But in the late 1960s and early 1970s oil supply became tight. The demand for oil by the United States, Western Europe and Japan increased astronomically. The oil companies were unable to discover new oil reserves to keep pace with the increasing demand of the United States, Western Europe and Japan. Oil became black gold and the prices for the various blends of oil began to rise.

In the early 1970s a number of negotiations took place between the oil companies and the oil producing countries at Tripoli, Baghdad and Geneva, indisputable evidence of the new status of oil. The discussions centred on how best to compensate the oil producing countries for depreciations in the value of the dollar, the currency in which oil prices were quoted. In 1971 the Smithsonian agreement revalued major world currencies except the US dollar. This in effect meant the devaluation of the dollar. Oil producing countries had to renegotiate oil prices to accommodate the depreciating value of the dollar. In 1973 when the dollar was properly devalued oil prices were again renegotiated to accommodate the devalued dollar. As a result of the devaluation of the dollar in 1973 the Organisation of Petroleum Exporting Countries (OPEC) announced the doubling of oil prices on 16 October 1973, to the enormous shock of the oil consuming nations. The main argument of OPEC member states in favour of the 100 per cent increase was the fact of raging inflation generated, it was alleged, by the trade unions of the industrialised countries. Inflationary pressures coupled with the depreciating dollar increased the import bills of OPEC member countries; hence the doubling of the barrel price of oil by OPEC.

While OPEC countries acted as a body the political constellation in the Middle East arising from the Arab/Israeli war of 1973 aggravated the oil situation. The conflict occurred about the time when the October price increases were announced. Arab member countries of OPEC decided on oil boycott measures against the West to retaliate for alleged help to Israel during the war. The organisation of Arab Petroleum Exporting Countries (OAPEC) consisting of Arab members of OPEC and Arab countries such as Bahrain, Dubai, Egypt and Syria then imposed the oil boycott on the United States and Holland. The boycott led to panic in the world oil markets and to speculative oil purchases. By December, 1973 oil prices were once again doubled. Between October and December 1973 oil prices quadrupled causing economic and financial constellations never imagined by the oil consuming countries. OPEC member countries suddenly discovered an important weapon for offence and defence in the modern world of international economic and power politics. Oil producing countries became so wealthy that countries which were once borrowers became lenders to the industrialised countries. Petrodollars were recycled into the economies of the advanced countries to ease their financial pressures. OPEC countries began to gain more foreign exchange through oil sales than they could afford to spend. Nigeria, a member of OPEC, experienced so much wealth that financial resources were no longer considered a constraint on national economic development. Nigerian imports increased to an unprecedented level and ostentatious living became the order of the day.

While the oil producing countries were swimming in wealth the industrialised countries found it difficult to balance their current accounts. The deficits in the current accounts of some of the industrialised countries became so staggering that the fear of recession lapsing into depression gripped those countries' leaders. The economic squeeze did not affect the industrialised countries only. The non-oil producing developing countries were probably the most hard hit. Countries such as India, Tanzania and Malawi, to name but a few, suffered tremendous economic hardship unknown in their countries' histories. Development plans could no longer be implemented and a number of projects were grounded. The industrialised countries on the other hand took a number of measures of a budgetary and tax nature to contain recession, reduce the level of unemployment and stimulate their economies. The economic and rational use of energy was stressed as there were as yet no viable alternatives to oil.

The new dimensions in world oil prices and politics emboldened OPEC member countries into stiffening their demands for active participation in the oil and allied industries. The forecast by the *Club of Rome* about the possible exhaustion of the world's major raw materials before the end of the present century frightened both oil producing and oil consuming countries. Oil became automatically defined as a very scarce commodity and oil producing countries began to demand unconditional participation in the planning, management and use of their scarce oil resources.

The oil multinationals, finding themselves for once in untenable positions, had no other option but to agree to such participation. While the Gulf oil producing states of OPEC accepted 25 per cent participation to begin with, Iran on the other hand took over all the operations of international companies in Iran. The National Iranian Oil Company conceded to the oil companies the role of production contractors with the privilege of buying oil for a term of 20 years. A part of the participatory agreement involved the governments of the oil producing countries acquiring some portions of oil produced in their countries for sale on the open market in order to derive more revenue than they could get from the oil companies in royalties and tax or by the oil companies buying back the government's own share of oil. OPEC as a body continued to object to the use of posted prices by the oil companies because of the difficulty of establishing the proper relationship between the costs of oil production and posted oil prices. OPEC therefore established any price it considered proper for the rich oil consuming countries. The reduction in oil output by 10 per cent by Arab members of OPEC and by the Arab non-OPEC members as the Arab/Israeli war continued led to a further squeeze in oil supply. Consequently oil which before 1971 was sold at about $3 per barrel rose on the open market to between $17 and $20 per barrel.

By 1974 the world's largest oil producer and the strongest member of OPEC, Saudi Arabia, began to buckle under pressure from the United States. The Saudis expressed the fear that if oil prices continued to rise this would lead to a reduction in the demand for oil and a quest for alternative energy sources by the industrialised countries. Any alternative source of energy would invariably affect the projected long-term use of Saudi Arabia's enormous oil reserves. Again, Saudi Arabia reasoned that worldwide economic recession might not save the long-term interests of both OPEC member countries and the industrialised countries. The shaky position of Saudi Arabia led to a drop in the price of oil from between $17 to $20 per barrel in the early months of 1974 to between $10 and $11 per barrel by mid-1974. Since 1974 Saudi Arabia has played a very important part in determining world oil market prices, particularly in the 1980s. The Saudi Arabian 'factor' in the oil glut of the 1980s has already been discussed.

Conservation is one remedy for the major oil consumers. A reasonable percentage of oil consumed by the industrialised countries is used for heating purposes. Research institutes in the United States and Europe were put in top gear to devise heat conservation technologies. Heat conservation is one of the cheapest means for cutting down on oil consumption. Insulation measures came into force. New buildings designed to incorporate insulation and thermostatic controls are now installed in homes and industries to regulate heating and airconditioning. Other suggestions to cut down on heating costs include draught-proofing, roof insulation, wall insulation, temperature standardisation and double glazing. These measures were expected to conserve over 15 per cent of oil used for the purpose of heating homes and industries as well as providing airconditioning for homes and offices, especially in summer.

Fiscal measures were devised to ensure that heat conservation was achieved. Differential tariffs were enforced in both the United States and Britain but in opposite directions. Public utilities in the United States made bulk rate adjustments upwards. The more one consumes the higher one pays. This measure is intended to discourage the wasteful use of heat. In the United Kingdom, on the other hand, the more one uses the less one pays after a given minimum. This does not encourage conservation and the measure is being criticised.

2. The Threat of Military Intervention

In the wake of rising oil prices and the recession in the economies of Western Europe and the United States, the United States under President Nixon threatened to intervene militarily, if need be, to ensure that oil continued to flow to the economies of the industrialised countries of the West. The threat showed the desperation both of the United States and her allies and indicated how badly the radical oil price policies of the oil producing countries were hurting Western economies. Whether that threat was real or whether it was intended to intimidate the oil producing countries into lowering oil prices and stepping up production is academic. The threat re-echoed the horrors of the British and American navies which bombarded the coast of Japan in the nineteenth century with the objective of opening up the Japanese market for European and American goods. It reminded the oil producing countries of a similar desperation on the part of the United States during World War II, when the Japanese invaded South East Asia cutting off the United States and her allies from rubber sources which were considered at the time of strategic potential for peace and war. The United States and her allies invaded South East Asia to dislodge, *inter alia*, the Japanese from their important political and strategic position in the area, and one of the major objectives was to capture a region endowed with a rich variety of raw materials.

Although the United States government has not directly intervened militarily there is evidence to suggest that it may be doing so indirectly. Despite the fact that the United States government and the revolutionary government of Iran are not on the best of terms, during the crucial period of the Iran/Iraq war the United States government was suspected to have given military assistance to Iran via Israel in return for extra oil production over and above the quota assigned to Iran by OPEC. The excess production was sold to the United States at a price below OPEC's reference price. The invasion of Iraq by Iran in July 1982 offered another opportunity for the United States and Israel. Two-fold objectives were expected to be achieved from the invasion: it would weaken Iraq, regarded as Israel's worst Arab enemy; Iran would be forced to produce over and above the OPEC allocation in order to earn foreign exchange for the purchase of arms required for the war against Iraq. The excess oil production by Iran over and above that allotted to it by OPEC would be purchased by the United States.

The United States government is diplomatically very active in the Middle East because of oil. It has sold an advanced reconnaissance aircraft to Saudi Arabia to warn against enemy intrusion into Saudi Arabian air space. This sophisticated aircraft, fitted with high-powered electronic equipment and called ARWAC (Advanced Radar Warning Aircraft) was meant to soften Saudi Arabia's position in OPEC and to portray the United States as a friend of the Saudis in peace, and in wartime. The threat by the Iranian government to escalate the war with Iraq to the Gulf States, including Saudi Arabia if necessary, has driven Saudi Arabia closer to the United States. The Saudi government, it appears, is ready to co-operate in the policy intentions of the United States. The threat by Saudi Arabia to flood the oil market in order to stabilise oil prices, if OPEC countries continued to raise oil prices, was intended to stampede OPEC into stabilising oil prices in the interests of the major oil consuming countries.

The United States is not directly involved in military operations in the Gulf region as was the case in South East Asia, but the tactics of playing one country against the other in the Gulf region has yielded enormous economic advantages for the United States.

3. Background of OPEC's Stand

How to bridge the gap in the standard of living between the rich industrialised countries and the raw material producing countries is a subject which has featured in international conferences since the 1940s. Many propositions have been put forward on how best to bridge the gap. The oldest of the proposals is economic aid. During the inauguration of President Truman of the United States in 1949 the problems of economic development for the poor nations were brought into the political limelight. It was believed that through a plan similar to that of General Marshall's which rebuilt war-battered Europe, the developing countries might also be helped to grow above the poverty line and to attain the same standard of living as the United States of America and Western Europe.

One can say that President Truman's Point IV Programme of 1949, though limited in its approach to global balancing of resources, formed the embryo from which today's theory of International Economic Order is growing into adulthood. Truman's programme was based on the Christian ideal of generosity to humanity so that poor nations might be converted to solvent trading partners and stable and peaceful members of the community of nations. The programme hardly gathered momentum before it lost its lustre. Western and Eastern politicians alike turned the policy into a subtle instrument of diplomacy.

The war of semantics was started in the guise of finding practical solutions to the problems of the countries of the 'Third World' group. In the 1950s and 1960s the issues were the proper definition and parameters for classifying the underprivileged group of countries. Should they be termed poor countries, backward countries, undeveloped nations, developing nations or underdeveloped nations? What level of *per capita* income should be required for a reclassification of a country from backward to developed?

Economic development became a major area of research in American and European universities. New theories emerged and classical international economic theories were revived. Visionary as some of them were in their approach to the development problems of the 'Third World', the arguments they raised sustained the debate on the economic prospects of poor countries. Some Western scholars appeared to concede that little could be done to help the poor countries as they were linked by a vicious circle of low productivity, poverty and poor capital formation.

While some scholars of the industrialised countries saw little economic prospects for 'Third World' countries, some scholars like Jan Tinbergen were full of optimism. Religiously the case of the 'Third

World' was argued. If the industrialised countries were to aid the developing countries with about 1 per cent of their GDP or at least with 0.76 per cent of it, the disparity in the standard of living between the advanced and the developing economies might be narrowed to a ratio of 6 to 1 within a few decades. The more ambitious goal of Tinbergen's group was to achieve a 3 to 1 relationship. This meant the slowing down of the rate of growth of the developed countries by 1.7 per cent *per annum* and the raising of the *per annum* growth rate of the developing countries to at least 5 per cent. Tinbergen's book, *Reshaping the World Economy* published in the late 1960s is the climax of his argument for shifting resources to 'Third World' countries. Tinbergen and his group were dubbed Utopians in much the same way that Malthus was referred to in his time. The optimism shown by Tinbergen led to a reassessment of the problems of developing countries.

While academics were arguing the pros and cons of economic development, politicians of the 'Third World' organised themselves. The first major meeting of the leaders of the developing countries was the Bandung Conference of 1955, said to be of as great a significance to the socialists of the twentieth century as the Communist Manifesto was to the socialists of the nineteenth century. Since the Bandung Conference, developing countries have closed ranks. Regional and supra-regional alliances have been formed with the objective of presenting a common front in matters affecting their political and economic destinies. In 1976 it was the group of 77; it has now grown to over 100 member countries. And earlier on, in 1960, OPEC had been formed.

The rapid increases in oil prices caused a political and economic crisis in the economically advanced countries. A number of other factors helped to jolt the industrialised countries from their slumber and from their false sense of security. In the late 1960s the Club of Rome had warned about the limits of growth and the necessity for a proper allocation of world resources. The recession of the 1960s, the crisis of the dollar and the pound sterling, the problems of gold shortage, inadequacy of world liquidity, the unruly political world of urban guerrillas and international air and sea piracies aroused the Western world from its complacency. For the first time the Western world realised that it was no longer in control of the situation. The economic crisis confronting it was structural and of an international nature. It was no longer prudent to attempt to combat such a crisis with classical or modified cyclical monetary and fiscal therapies. A new and bolder policy dimension was necessary which could only be found in the context of world politics, economics and society: a new International Order which will allow for a fair allocation of world resources, of self-determination and of respect for cultural diversity is imperative. Eurocentrism and Atlantocentrism must give way to a *New World Order*. The era of gunboat diplomacy was surely over. 'Small' countries can no longer be intimidated into surrendering their resources without due compensation. Equitable resource sharing can only be hammered out in a general setting of International Economic Order.

A new International Economic Order was accordingly enunciated at the Seventh Special Session of the United Nations General Assembly in 1975. Several negotiations and conferences have taken place since then including the 'North-South Dialogue'.

4. International Trade

The exportable commodities of most African economies are inelastic and bedevilled with price instability. Prices of raw materials such as cocoa, cotton, palm kernels, palm oil, timber, sisal, coffee and groundnuts are fixed through bilateral agreements. On the other hand prices of imports continue to rise bcause of the accelerating cost of various factors — especially labour costs — in advanced economies. The conflicting situation of rising import prices and falling export prices very adversely affects the balance of payments position of the developing African countries and their terms of trade.

Development economists appear to be unanimous in their view that the pattern of trade between the developed and the developing countries explains, in the final analysis, the differences in the *per capita* income or in the standard of living between the advanced and the developing economies. Conversely, the polarisation in the standard of living is due to differences in technological concentration or technological gaps. Countries which produce agricultural goods and raw materials experience a lower standard of living while those that produce engineering goods experience a higher standard of living. There is therefore a causal relationship between the degree of technological concentration or engineering capability and *per capita* income.

The nature of production influences both the pattern of trade and the terms of trade. While the exports of the advanced economies are highly elastic and respond well to changing world incomes and inflationary indices, those of the developing countries, with the exception of certain mineral resources, are inelastic and respond poorly to changing world economic conditions. The terms of trade between the advanced countries and the developing countries continue to deteriorate to the net disadvantage of the peripheral developing economies, because the import packets of the developing economies consist mainly of engineering goods, equipment and manufactures which they themselves cannot produce. The import packets from the advanced economies have strong agglomerative pulls on their incomes and resources.

Sensing the damaging effect of the pattern of trade between them and the industrialised countries, independent Third World countries convened the Havana Conference in 1948, to discuss international trade inequalities and their remedies. When the Havana Conference was still being planned, a number of industrialised countries hurriedly met in 1947, formed GATT (General Agreement on Tariffs and Trade) and agreed to grant trade concessions among themselves on reciprocal bases, excluding the developing countries who lacked the capacity to concede trade on reciprocal terms, but who rather sought some trade concessions. The EEC and other regional economic associations of the industrialised countries also excluded the developing countries from full participation. Efforts have been made by the United Nations through UNCTAD (United Nations Commission for Trade and Development) to find a just solution to the problems of world trade. These efforts have not yielded any meaningful result, notwithstanding the so-called 'North-South Dialogue'.

The advanced countries would like to solve the problems of development through aid. The developing countries on the other hand want better trade terms. Their experiences with foreign aid have been bitter ones. Aid *per se* can be very inadequate. The cost of servicing the aid has been found to be prohibitive. An aid-receiving country is forced to spend most of the loan on the purchase of equipment, machinery, plant, tools or other requirements from the producers of the aid-giving country, even where the receiving country could afford to buy cheaper on the open market. Besides the compulsory purchase, the receiving country is compelled to ship the machinery or equipment with the carrier of the donor country. Finally donor-country engineers or technicians must be hired at prohibitive costs to install the machinery and to operate it for an agreed period, even when the engineers of the receiving country are capable of making the installation without outside assistance.

The reactions of the oil producing countries to oil prices can be seen in the light of the above historical development in international co-operation between the Third World countries and the industrial-ised countries. Third World countries have sought for better trade relations and better prices for their products over the decades in the conviction that they stood to gain more through better trade terms than through economic aid. The present world oil situation has offered the oil producing states in particular all the chances they have sought for years. Oil is the only weapon available to them now. They have to make the best use of it to recover the trade losses of the past and to acquire much needed funds for their development.

5. OPEC in Disarray

Because of the world oil glut there was a fear of overproduction among OPEC members and a realisation of the danger of market forces pushing down OPEC's reference prices for the various blends of oil. To arrest the situation OPEC member countries met at Quito early in 1982 and agreed on production ceilings for members whereby OPEC's total oil production was set at 17.5 million barrels a day. The output level was shared among OPEC members according to an agreed ratio based on the oil production of OPEC member countries over the preceding ten years (see Table 6.1).

However when member countries met in Vienna in July, 1982 to review the allocations, there was serious disagreement on future oil pricing and production policies. For the first time OPEC could no longer speak with one voice. Iran refused to continue with the pro-duction quota of 1.2 million barrels per day allocated to her during the Quito meeting of March, 1982. War-torn Iran argued that coun-tries such as Saudi Arabia and Iraq should limit their production to allow Iran to step up her quota in order to overcome the problems of a country suffering the after effects of revolution and war. The Iranian Oil Minister insisted that the gentleman's agreement reached at the Quito meeting be kept. According to the Iranian Minister it was agreed that Iran would be allowed in future to increase her quota in order to restore her war-torn economy and to rebuild the Iranian cities destroyed during the Iran/Iraq war. Other member countries, notably Venezuela, disputed the Iranian viewpoint. Arab member countries were also in opposition although the opposition was not outwardly pronounced. The Iranian Minister proposed another element in the production sharing guidelines. He argued that future production quotas should be based on population. The new criterion proposed by Iran took other members by surprise and could have earned the support of populous oil countries such as Nigeria. Iran could not understand why Saudi Arabia with only 10 million people is allowed to export about 8 million barrels a day while Iran with 38 million people is allowed only 1.2 million barrels a day. The opinion of the Iranian Oil Minister was disputed by Saudi Arabia and Iraq. Many OPEC members supported the call that Saudi Arabia should reduce her quota below 7.5 million barrels a day, which Saudi Arabia had volunteered at Quito in March, 1982. However, Saudi Arabia proposed a doubling of the fixed $1.50 price differential between the high quality sweet crude produced by countries such as Nigeria, Algeria and Libya and the Saudi Arabian blend. The three African countries were accused of overproducing and of selling oil at discount prices. The price differential made the African sweet crude more expensive by $1.50 as against the Saudi Arabian price. If doubled then the African sweet crude would be more expensive than the Saudi Arabian crude by $3. The African oil producing countries vehemently opposed the Saudi Arabian proposal on the ground that the prices of their crudes were already selling above their spot market rates.

The current disagreement among OPEC members is bound to have some repercussions on the organisation's pricing policy. The disagreement was so intense that deliberation had to be suspended for the first time in the history of the organisation. By suspending deliberations the organisation unwittingly invited a free-for-all oil policy. This was a situation which Saudi Arabia had hoped would materialise so that she could pursue a production policy consistent with her avowed long-term aim of pushing down oil prices and containing any recession which could be harmful to the United States and to other Western nations, where Saudi Arabia has invested billions of dollars of oil money. The undeclared price war among members will certainly, in the absence of a common production policy, push aggregate production above the 17.5 million barrels a day mark agreed in March, 1982. This will obviously create another oil glut and lead to price cutting among OPEC members.

After the Quito meeting, Saudi Arabia volunteered a soft loan of about $2 billion to Nigeria to enable her to overcome her economic squeeze — a consequence of the oil glut. The offer was made to push Nigeria into accepting future cuts in her quota so that Saudi Arabia might increase her own quota. Nigeria was unaware of the motive behind the offer. When Nigeria eventually wanted to take up the offer, the Saudi Arabians were no longer so keen when they realised that Nigeria would accept neither any further cut in her quota nor any proposal to increase the price differential between African crude and Saudi Arabian crude. From Nigeria's stand during the Vienna meeting there is little hope that Nigeria will ever receive any soft loan from Saudi Arabia. Through conservation measures the industrialised countries have been able to reduce consumption by seven million barrels a day. Instead of 52.4 million barrels a day, consumption has dropped to about 45 million barrels a day. OPEC's position has been made more difficult by the oil policies of Mexico, Britain and Norway which are not strictly tied to those of OPEC. Shortly after the Vienna meeting the estimated demand for OPEC oil for the period July to September, 1982, was between 18.5 million and 19.5 million barrels a day. The estimate is higher than the Quito production ceiling. Demand for the last quarter of the year (1982) is estimated at between 21.5 and 22.5 million barrels per day. If the estimates are correct, then OPEC member countries still have an opportunity to mend fences and adjust production quotas to the satisfaction of hard-pressed members. An adjustment of production quotas in the light of new forecasts is favoured by Saudi Arabia, which is interested in stabilising oil prices at $34 a barrel by additional oil production. However, most member countries, particularly Algeria, Venezuela and Libya insist that the present ceiling be maintained so that at the new estimated demand for OPEC oil prices will rise rather than stabilise at $34, as suggested by Saudi Arabia. The renewed fighting between Iraq and Iran in July, 1982, is bound to lead to speculative production and price cuts which may make agreement among OPEC members much more difficult.

6. OPEC and Non-Oil Producing Third World Countries

The oil policy of OPEC against the major consumers of oil does not only disagreeably affect major consumers but also has its effect on Third World countries which are not industrialised and which do not produce oil themselves. While the industrialised countries are able to reschedule investments from oil consuming sectors to other sectors, and while austerity measures can be effectively enforced using efficient systems set up for that purpose, it is practically impossible for Third World countries to adjust to the world economic crisis by shifting investments from one sector to another and to apply those disciplines essential for energy conservation, which the industrialised countries have acquired over the years.

The majority of the population of Third World countries lives below the poverty (or the bread) line. Increases in oil prices have affected the economies of the developing countries and pushed the standard of living of the people even further down the poverty line. Exports of Third World countries have dwindled over the years because of poor demand and prices for their raw materials. The export earnings of these countries have not been adequate for their planned development programmes. Aid from the industrialised countries to the Third World now only trickles. In some cases the sources of aid have dried up. The inadequacy of aid coupled with the poor export earnings of Third World countries have made it extremely difficult for them to sustain imports of machinery, equipment, plant and fertiliser required for their development plans. Other infrastructural developments such as roads, railways, seaports, airports, power supply and communications which are the *conditio sine qua non* for any meaningful development and economic growth have in some cases ground to a halt. The programmed growth rates of Third World countries which in the past have fallen short of expectation have worsened because of the negative impact of oil on their import bills and the high prices of other imports from the major industrialised countries.

In 1973 the total oil import bills of the less developed countries amounted to about $5 billion. By the end of 1974, oil import bills had risen to $15 billion with the volume of imports only slightly increasing. The high oil import bills of 1974 are the direct result of increased oil prices in the period. In the same period the total aid from official sources to the less developed countries amounted to $8 billion, an amount less than the difference between oil import bills of 1973 and 1974. Some less developed countries have been able to overcome the economic shock from rising oil prices because of their ability to satisfy some of their domestic demands from local production. These countries are Brazil, Argentina, Brunei, Malaysia and India. Other countries produce raw materials which are in demand. Ivory Coast and Cameroon, for example, produce cocoa; Tanzania produces sisal; Cuba and some West Indian countries produce sugar; southeast Asian countries produce rubber; Zambia produces copper while Mauritania and Morocco produce phosphate. These raw materials are some of the few which are still in demand in the world market and their prices are relatively elastic. Countries with such raw materials have more capacity to earn foreign exchange which reduces the hardships imposed by rising oil prices.

The most hard-hit countries are Pakistan, Sri Lanka, Bangladesh and African countries such as Uganda, Somalia, Ethiopia, Malawi, Central African Republic, Ruwanda, Chad, Ghana, Sierra Leone, Togo, Benin Republic, and the Gambia. These countries which do not produce oil and which do not have a strong export base have no other alternative but to go into direct bilateral oil arrangements with the governments of the oil producing countries of OPEC, and also by making use of the IMF oil facility arrangement and by seeking soft loans from willing lenders.

The OPEC organisation is no less concerned about the consequences of its oil pricing policy on the economies of the less developed countries. At the 56th OPEC conference in Caracas in 1979 one of the subjects discussed was how to accord priority to developing countries so that they can secure oil supplies for their domestic requirements on the basis of official prices instead of going through the oil majors for their oil needs.

As a follow-up, many non-oil-producing developing countries have developed strong relationships with the governments of OPEC member countries. To improve the concessional oil supplies to the less developed countries regional arrangements have also been made. In Central America, Venezuela and Mexico have adopted concessional oil supply policies to accommodate the non-oil producing countries of Central America. African member countries of OPEC have also entered into bilateral concessional oil supply arrangements between them and other African countries. Apart from the regional arrangements, any developing country which imports oil is free to enter into direct arrangements with any OPEC member country irrespective of the region of origin.

There has been an increase in economic co-operation between OPEC member countries and other developing countries which are non-members. This economic co-operation is centred mainly in the area of trade. By 1973 developing countries' exports to OPEC member countries approximated $3.5 billion. By 1979 this figure had grown to about $15.5 billion. The senior OPEC member, Saudi Arabia, increased her imports from other developing countries from $586 million in 1973 to $3.6 billion in 1979. The major beneficiaries of the increased exports from the developing countries to OPEC member countries have been South Korea and Taiwan. Apart from the growth in visible trade, remittances earned in OPEC member countries by immigrant workers from other developing countries have grown significantly. Countries such as India, Pakistan, Egypt and Bangladesh and a few other Asian countries gained from such remittances. According to IMF statistics total remittances were $1.26 billion in 1974 and $5.33 billion in 1977. By 1975, 1.5 million migrant workers from developing countries were estimated to be working in OPEC Middle East countries. The number was expected to have doubled by 1980. About two million migrant workers work in other OPEC member countries not situated in the Middle East. In Nigeria, for example, ECOWAS (Economic Community of West African States) migrant workers who left their countries because of the poor economic and political situations to work in Nigeria are estimated at about 500,000. While the majority of the migrant workers possess no skills a good number of them have skills in the areas of consultancy and construction. A large proportion of the construction works in Iran, Iraq and Kuwait are carried out by contractors of Third World countries. The same trend appears in Libya, Saudi Arabia and the United Arab Emirates.

Bilateral aid between OPEC member countries and oil importing developing countries has increased over the years. As far back as 1960 the Kuwait Fund for Arab Economic Development (KFAED) was established to provide soft loans to Arab states based on proper project evaluation and without taking into consideration the political ideology of the recipient country. The initial capital was $600 million and by 1974 it had risen to $3.3 billion with a borrowing authority of an extra $12 billion. The organisation was renamed Kuwait Fund for Economic Development (KFED) and was made open to both Arab and non-Arab developing countries. Some African countries benefited from the scheme in the late 1970s.

Saudi Arabia, the richest of the OPEC member countries, has also generated an assistance programme, especially in the Arab world. Saudi Arabia has provided soft loans to Egypt and liberation funds to Arab freedom fighters such as the PLO. Saudi Arabia has also extended assistance to some African countries such as Uganda (during the dictatorship of President Dada Idi Amin). Iran has provided aid to Pakistan and India for the development of industrial projects. In the case of India the loan is repaid over a long time with the products of the industries financed with the long-term loan from Iran. In Africa, Nigeria has provided funds to the African Development Bank (ADB) and participates in iron mining in the Republic of

Guinea. Nigeria has also provided financial assistance to the Benin Republic and Angola, to name but a few. Apart from bilateral financial assistance to developing countries, OPEC countries subscribe to the funds of the International Bank for Reconstruction and Development (IBRD) to help the non-oil-producing countries to borrow under more favourable conditions.

The total aid provided by OPEC countries since 1973 is more than two per cent of the total GNP of OPEC member countries. On the other hand the industrialised countries have not been able to provide up to 0.7 per cent of their GNP for the purposes of providing financial aid to the developing countries in keeping with the United Nation's plan for the second development decade. In addition to bilateral and multilateral arrangements, the OPEC Fund For International Development with capital of over $4 billion has provided assistance to over 80 developing countries.

References and Additional Reading

'A Hysterical World Oil Situation', in the *Business Times*, Lagos, 12 June 1979

'Borrowing in a Difficult Climate', in the *Financial Punch*, Lagos, 29 March 1982

Feyide, M.O., 'Economics of Oil Politics', Speech at the Tenth Nigerian Institute of Journalism Annual Seminar, published in *NAPETCOR*, vol. 3, no. 1, Jan.-March, 1982

'Increased Demand From OPEC Oil', in the *Business Times*, Lagos, 15 July 1982

'Nigeria and Oil Diplomacy', in the *Daily Times*, Lagos, 2 Oct. 1981

'Nigeria Should Stick with OPEC', in the *Punch*, Lagos, 5 April 1982

'OPEC and Other Developing Countries', in the *National Concord*, Lagos, 17 July 1982

'OPEC, Oil Companies — A Show of Strength', in the *Business Times*, Lagos, 10 May 1982

'OPEC Wins Price Battle', in the *Business Times*, Lagos, 17 May 1982

'$1b Loan From Saudi Unlikely', in the *Business Times*, Lagos, 15 July 1982

'Scenario: What if there had been no OPEC', in the *Financial Punch*, Lagos, 19 April 1982

'Towards a Rational Debt Policy for Nigeria', in the *Financial Punch*, Lagos, 5 April 1982

'The Western Blackmail of OPEC', in the *Punch*, Lagos, 21 April 1982

'Saudi Arabia, Kuwait and Quatar Offer ₦670m Loan', in the *Business Times*, Lagos, 29 March 1982

'Why Gold has Joined Oil in Eclipse', in the *Nigerian Statesman*, Owerri, 26 April 1982

'Who is to Blame for Instability in Oil Industry', in the *Business Times*, Lagos, 17 May 1982

9   OPEC — TO BE OR NOT TO BE?

For over two decades OPEC proved to be the most formidable raw material cartel ever formed by a group of developing countries. Until recently it ably withstood international economic and political forces aimed at disintegrating the unity of the organisation.

In the last few years however, the organisation has experienced a number of cracks on its walls. Forces which tend to act against the very existence of OPEC are many. These forces have already been examined in earlier chapters. While some of these forces acting on OPEC are endogenous, others are exogenous to OPEC. The most devastating force is the force of disunity which has threatened OPEC as a result of differences generated by the oil glut which has been an intermittent factor since 1977 but which reached its climax in the 1981/2 period. The unanimity for which OPEC has been known in the areas of price fixing and output quota in order to maintain OPEC's agreed reference price is apparently a thing of the past. OPEC member countries are now completely disorganised in a manner that defeats the very purpose of its existence. OPEC has degenerated into an organisation with an open-ended policy in which members push their selfish interests to the detriment of more general interests.

At the international level many questions are being raised. Can OPEC survive the turmoil within its rank and file? In view of the recent developments in the oil business the rationale of Nigeria continuing as a member of OPEC is being questioned. Opinions are divided. Some are of the opinion that Nigeria is a weak link in the OPEC equation and that Nigeria may be crushed by the weight of the heavier member nations especially those of the Gulf States. More enlightened opinions argue that the best way to ruin Nigeria's oil economy is by withdrawing from membership of OPEC and through oil price cuts to achieve more sales. The opponents of Nigeria's continuous membership in OPEC are of the view that by Nigeria's withdrawal she will no longer be bound by OPEC's tight quota at a time when Nigeria badly needs foreign exchange. Nigeria stood to gain as a member on the one hand and lose on the other by opting out of the organisation. The benefits of membership by far outweigh the current problems of Nigeria resulting from OPEC membership.

1. Benefits of OPEC to Member Countries

The old adage, 'unity is strength', still holds good for OPEC inspite of its present problems. Through unity OPEC members have been able to destroy the monopoly status of the seven international oil majors who in the past exploited the oil resources of OPEC member countries, paying what amounted to token rents and royalties and refusing any participation by the governments of those countries in the oil industry. In the absence of any suitable alternative, the oil majors continued to operate with impunity. Through unity of purpose OPEC member countries are now participating in petroleum production and refining and in other allied industries such as gas. A break-up of OPEC will open up the flanks once more for the oil majors, who have been waiting on the side lines for over a decade to start a fresh manoeuvre for monopoly in order to play their former roles. The oil majors fully appreciate what they have lost over the years in terms of extra income and transfer of oil technology to the developing countries. Should they find themselves once more in the position of power, as was the case in the 1940s, the 1950s and 1960s, they will do everything possible to make it impossible for the oil producing countries to retrieve the powers lost to the oil companies because of their disunity. This fact is recognised even by the strongest and most benevolent member of OPEC, Saudi Arabia, whose recent role tended to weaken, more than strengthen, OPEC unity. Saudi Arabia is still reluctant to see OPEC disintegrate.

By coming together OPEC member countries have been able to co-ordinate and unify petroleum prices. From $0.18 per barrel of oil in 1960 the price of oil per barrel reached the bench mark of about $41 in 1982. This price level would have been unattainable, if OPEC member countries had entered the oil market as competitors. OPEC still maintains a monopolistic position in the world oil market as it produces over 60 per cent of the world's oil needs. Its position as a monopolist has helped it fix oil prices which are consistent with the inflationary prices of imported manufactured goods from the industrialised countries and enabled it to match the established prices with the appropriate production quota for the entire members of the organisation. Through unified policies the interests of member countries have been fully protected.

Debtor members of OPEC such as Nigeria, Iran, Indonesia, Venezuela, Iraq and Algeria have been able to redeem their international images and restore their credit standing. They have been able to embark on their development programmes more realistically as funds which in the past constituted an insurmountable bottleneck had ceased to be a major constraining factor. Countries like Libya and Kuwait which have been net creditors have also benefited from rising oil prices. In Libya surplus oil money which can no longer be conveniently absorbed in the economy is being used to finance military adventures in Africa and in the Middle East and to prop up revolutionary forces wherever a fertile ground shows itself. In countries like Saudi Arabia, Qatar and the United Arab Emirates which have an enormous surplus of oil money, the excess oil money is being invested in the assets of the industrialised countries thereby recycling the petroleum dollar. The income gains which are a direct product of OPEC unity are too significant to be ignored in the vital decision as to whether OPEC survives — or dies a quick death.

OPEC members also derive benefits in the area of research, specialised technical advice, technological transfer, manpower development and world economic analyses by pooling their resources together. Through the exchange of programmes OPEC members have benefited immensely from the experiences of member nations at very little cost. Newcomers like Nigeria, as yet still backward in oil technology, stand to gain more from the above areas of co-operation.

Another argument in favour of OPEC's continued existence is the development funds the organisation makes available to 45 African, Asian, Latin American and Caribbean countries. OPEC also contributes directly and indirectly to other international organisations from which the developing countries of Asia, Africa, Latin America, and the Caribbean can borrow on very easy terms. OPEC's co-operation with Third World countries has already been discussed in the preceding chapter.

2. The Middle East Geopolitical Factor

In Chapter eight the forces emanating from OPEC with respect to the July, 1982 Vienna conference were discussed. But there is an aspect which requires more emphasis here and which can be termed the most immediate threatening factor to OPEC's existence. This is Middle East geopolitics. While OPEC in the past took advantage of Middle East crises such as the Arab/Israeli war of 1973 to raise oil prices to OPEC's benefit, the struggle by the Middle Eastern countries of OPEC such as Iran, Saudi Arabia and Iraq to assert political and military supremacy in the Gulf region will invariably harm OPEC more than the other forces which are external to it.

During the era of the late Shah of Iran the supremacy of Iran in the Persian Gulf was incontrovertible. Iran's military might, her second position in the OPEC league and the peacock flamboyancy of the late Shah of Iran projected the Iranian nation to the forefront of international politics, a posture which by far outshone the Arab Gulf States of Saudi Arabia, Iraq and other minor States of the Gulf region. The military superiority of Iran over her Arab neighbours and the modernisation of the Iranian economy as against the feudal nature of the Arab economies of the Gulf region made Iran assume the role of gendarme to protect the Gulf region against communist influence.

With the overthrow of the Shah of Iran in 1978 and the struggle for power within Iran itself, the unique Iranian position in the Gulf region was lost. A vacuum was created which Iraq was determined to fill and at the same time assert herself as the power of the region. Iraq was also determined to avenge the humiliation suffered by Arab nations under the hands of the Iranians and to reclaim Arab lands allegedly taken over by Iran through conquest. In 1981, Iraq invaded Iran and annexed Iranian territories which Iraq claimed to be Arab lands. A revolution-torn Iran once more became united in the fight against a common enemy, Iraq. After over a year of Iraqi occupation of Iranian territories the Iranian army succeeded in pushing back the Iraqi forces. After recovering their territories, Iran carried the war into Iraqi territory and demanded the overthrow of President Hussein of Iraq and reparation of over $150 billion in return for a cessation by Iran of her counter-invasion against Iraq. The ultimate objective of the Iranian Ayatollah Khomeini is to create a Shiite nation through a forced amalgamation of Iran and Iraq. The Shiites are the predominant Moslem group in Iran and Iraq. If Iraq is secured then the way would be paved to fight Israel, the common enemy of Moslem countries.

The struggle between Iran and Iraq will certainly affect the very existence of OPEC. The Vienna drama was a pointer to the dangers the presence of combatant member nations would pose to the organisation. Iranian cities, especially those in the border areas, have been destroyed and both Iranian and Iraqi oil installations have been damaged. To rebuild the shattered economies of both countries, notably that of Iran, would demand enormous foreign exchange earnings. In the circumstances it was unlikely that Iran or Iraq would accept the quota allocated to them by OPEC. The crisis at the Vienna conference was the consequence of Iran's insistence to be allowed to produce at least three million barrels per day contrary to the 1.5 million barrels allocated to her. Iran also insisted that the 1.5 million barrels per day extra allocation be deducted from the 7.5 million barrels a day allocated to Saudi Arabia and the 1.2 million barrels a day allocated to the enemy, Iraq. It is most unlikely that either Saudi Arabia or Iraq would agree to the Iranian proposals. Iran was also embittered by a report that Saudi Arabia in conjunction with Kuwait provided soft loans amounting to $20 billion to Iraq to enable her partly to overcme the stress caused to her economy by the war against Iran and partly to enable Iraq to prosecute the war successfully against Iran. Although President Sadam Hussein of Iraq is considered a revolutionary and therefore a danger to feudalist Saudi Arabia, to Saudi Arabia Hussein is a lesser evil compared to the revolutionary Ayatollah Khomeini. Khomeini's brand of revolution can wipe out the monarchical system of Saudi Arabia as it did that of Persia.

The Middle East geopolitical factor poses to a large extent a greater threat to OPEC than probably other forces external to OPEC. So long as the Middle Eastern countries continue to jockey for military and political supremacy in the Gulf region, the unity of OPEC as demonstrated since the 1960s until the early 1980s will remain an illusion.

References and Additional Reading

Abolfathi, F. *et al.*, *The OPEC Market to 1985*, DC Heath and Co., Lexington, Mass., 1977

'A Collapse of OPEC Unity', in the *Newsweek*, Lagos, 1982

Akinbobola, A., *Should Nigeria Be in OPEC?*, Nigerian Institute of International Affairs Monograph Series, 1979

Kubbah, A.A., *OPEC Past and Present*, Petro-Economic Research Centre, Vienna, Sep., 1974

Middle East Economic Survey, Middle East Petroleum and Economic Publications, Nicosia, Cyprus, (Weekly)

'Middle East Geo-Politics Threatens OPEC Solidarity', in the *Financial Punch*, Lagos, 26 July 1982

Monroe, Elizabeth (ed.), *The Changing Balance of Power in the Persian Gulf*, The American Universities Field Staff, Inc., New York, 1982

'Nigeria Should Stick with OPEC', in the *Punch*, Lagos, 5 April 1982

'OPEC After Vienna: The New Reality', in the *Financial Punch*, Lagos, 29 March 1982

'OPEC Deficit Looms Large', in the *Financial Punch*, Lagos, 26 April 1982

'OPEC: Oil Companies — A Show of Strength', in the *Business Times*, Lagos, 10 May 1982

OPEC Review, Public Relations Department, Organization of Petroleum Exporting Countries, Vienna

'OPEC: Victory or Defeat?', in the *Business Times*, Lagos, 26 April 1982

'OPEC Wins Price Battle', in the *Business Times*, Lagos, 31 May 1982

Petroleum Economist, Petroleum Press Bureau Ltd., London, (Monthly)

Petroleum Intelligence Weekly, Petroleum and Energy Intelligence Weekly Inc., New York

Sadik, Muhammed T. and William P. Snavely, *Bahrain, Qatar, and the United Arab Emirates*, DC Heath and Company, Lexington, Mass., 1972

'Scenario: What If There Had Been No OPEC', in the *Financial Punch*, Lagos, 19 April 1982

'The Nigerian Oil Conundrum: Three Scenarios and the Implications for 1983', in the *Financial Punch*, Lagos, 26 July 1982

'The Western Blackmail of OPEC', in the *Punch*, Lagos, 21 April 1982

Tokuma, R.A., *OPEC and NIEO: A Strategy of Change*, Nigerian Institute of International Affairs, Sept., 1977

'Who is to Blame for Instability in the Oil Industry', in the *Business Times*, Lagos, 17 May 1982

INDEX

148

For Product Safety Concerns and Information please contact our EU
representative GPSR@taylorandfrancis.com Taylor & Francis Verlag GmbH,
Kaufingerstraße 24, 80331 München, Germany

Printed and bound by CPI Group (UK) Ltd, Croydon, CR0 4YY
08/05/2025
01864392-0001